WITHDRAWN

Charles Williams

Twayne's English Authors Series

Kinley E. Roby, Editor

Northeastern University

TEAS 322

CHARLES WILLIAMS
(1886–1945)
Photograph kindly lent by the Charles
Williams Society and used by permission
of Faber and Faber

Charles Williams

By Agnes Sibley

Twayne Publishers • *Boston*

Charles Williams

Agnes Sibley

Copyright © 1982
Twayne Publishers
A Division of G. K. Hall & Company
70 Lincoln Street
Boston, Massachusetts 02111

Book production by Marne B. Sultz

Book design by Barbara Anderson

Printed on permanent/durable acid-free
paper and bound in The United States
of America.

Library of Congress Cataloging in
Publication Data

Sibley, Agnes Marie, 1914–1979.
    Charles Williams.

    (Twayne's English authors series ;
TEAS 322)
    Bibliography: p. 155
    Includes index.
    1.   Williams, Charles, 1886–1945.
—Criticism and interpretation.
I. Title. II. Series.
PR6045.I5Z89   1982   828'.91209   81–6676
ISBN 0–8057–6811–4   AACR2

Contents

About the Author

Agnes Sibley was born in Missouri but spent her childhood in the mining district of northeast Oklahoma, where her father was a physician. She received her B.A. and M.A. degrees from the University of Oklahoma. Her M.A. thesis was on John Donne and T. S. Eliot. Her Ph.D. degree was from Columbia University, where in 1946–47 she held the Lizette Andrews Fisher Fellowship in the Department of English and Comparative Literature. Her doctoral dissertation, *Alexander Pope's Prestige in America, 1725–1835,* was published by the King's Crown Press in 1949.

Her first teaching post was at Cottey College in Nevada, Missouri, but the greater part of her teaching career was at Lindenwood College (now the Lindenwood Colleges), St. Charles, Missouri, which she joined in 1943, and where she became Associate Professor of English until her retirement in 1974. In 1965 she was chosen as Faculty Lecturer and delivered an address (privately printed) on *Paradox and Poetic Truth.*

In 1951 she went to England as an exchange teacher under the Fulbright program and lectured in English literature at Bishop Otter College of Education, Chichester, Sussex. She prolonged her stay for a second year and later returned to Sussex for sabbatical leave and finally made her residence there when she retired.

Her experiences while at Bishop Otter College were published in 1961 by the Caxton Printers Ltd., Caldwell, Idaho, under the title *Exchange Teacher.*

In 1972 her literary study of *May Sarton* was published in Twayne's United States Authors Series.

She wrote *Charles Williams* in England, completing it shortly before her death from cancer in May 1979. She was fortunate in making contact in England with an enthusiastic group of former pupils of Charles Williams, who have formed a society for the study of his writings, and so she was able to draw upon their first-hand knowledge of him.

Preface

To mention Charles Williams is often to receive a puzzled look or a query as to who he was. Yet he is one of the most original and spiritually perceptive authors of our time. When he died in 1945, he was mourned not only by well-known religious writers such as C. S. Lewis, T. S. Eliot, and Dorothy Sayers, but by many others who found in his novels, poetry, and drama an awareness of greater life. His writings are not always easy, but for those who are willing to make an effort, the reward is great. He puts into fresh, contemporary language the age-old truths about God, the soul, the mystic experience, sin and salvation. Readers find in his works, not an escape from ordinary living, but an increasing understanding of its significance in eternal terms. W. H. Auden, who knew Williams, has mentioned him as one of the two people who could be called modern saints (the other is Dorothy Day). Yet Williams did not live a secluded life, and his religious faith was accompanied by constant questioning and skepticism. He was one of the first in England to recognize the importance of Søren Kierkegaard, and one critic has called Williams a Christian existentialist.

The purpose of the present study is to discuss the major creative works of Williams so as to make them available to more readers than they are at present. The poetry, which might especially present difficulties, is treated in most detail. After the first chapter, which gives the main facts of Williams's life and surveys the scope of his entire work and his chief ideas, his drama is discussed in Chapter 2, his novels in Chapter 3, and his poetry in Chapter 4. The last chapter attempts to summarize his achievement as an author and his significance in English literature.

I am greatly indebted to Alice Mary Hadfield, whose book, *An Introduction to Charles Williams,* was a constant source of reference. Mrs. Hadfield also read portions of the manuscript and gave me valuable criticism. I should add, however, that any errors in fact or interpretation are entirely my own. The meetings of the Charles

Williams Society in London, of which Mrs. Hadfield was a founder member, have been not only helpful to me but consistently enjoyable.

Agnes Sibley

Chronology

1886	Charles Walter Stansby Williams born in London, September 20.
1894	Moved with parents to St. Albans.
1898–1902	St. Albans Grammar School.
1901	Confirmation in St. Albans Abbey, March 27.
1902–1904	University College, London.
1904	Assistant in the Bookroom, Holborn; studied at Working Men's College, Crowndale Road.
1908–1939	Work at the Oxford University Press, London. Continued when the Press was evacuated to Oxford, 1939.
1912	*The Silver Stair*, poetry.
1917	Marriage to Florence Conway. *Poems of Conformity*.
1920	*Divorce*, poetry.
1923	Lecturing at London County Council Literary Institute.
1925	*Windows of Night*, poetry.
1927	*The Masque of the Manuscript*, drama.
1928	*The Myth of Shakespeare*, drama.
1929	*The Masque of Perusal*, drama.
1930	*Heroes and Kings*, poetry; *War in Heaven*, novel; *Poetry at Present*, criticism.
1931	*Three Plays*, drama; *Many Dimensions*, novel; *The Place of the Lion*, novel.
1932	*The Greater Trumps*, novel; *The English Poetic Mind*, criticism.
1933	*Shadows of Ecstasy*, novel; *Bacon*, biography; *Reason and Beauty in the Poetic Mind*, criticism.
1934	*James I*, biography.
1935	*Rochester*, biography.
1936	*Thomas Cranmer of Canterbury*, drama; *Queen Elizabeth*, biography.
1937	*Descent into Hell*, novel; *Henry VII*, biography.

1938	*Taliessin through Logres,* poetry; *He Came Down from Heaven,* theology.
1939	Removed to Southfield House, Oxford, with the staff of the Oxford University Press for the duration of the war. *Judgement at Chelmsford,* drama; *The Descent of the Dove, A Short History of the Holy Spirit in the Church,* theology.
1941	*Witchcraft,* theology.
1942	*The Forgiveness of Sins,* theology.
1943	Received honorary M.A. degree from Oxford University. *The Figure of Beatrice. A Study in Dante,* criticism.
1943–1945	Lecturing at Oxford University.
1944	*The Region of the Summer Stars,* poetry.
1945	Death May 15; *The House of the Octopus,* drama; *All Hallows' Eve,* novel.

Chapter One
The Man and His Ideas

Charles Williams led an outwardly uneventful life. He never took a holiday, and only once did he leave England, to give a lecture in Paris. It was as if he needed no external stimulus to make life interesting; an inner excitement about ideas carried him through what some would have regarded as boring days.

He was born in London on September 20, 1886. When he was eight years old his father was forced to leave his work and move out of London because of failing eyesight. The family settled in St. Albans, within commuting distance of London, where his mother opened an artists' supply shop, and they managed on the small income it brought in. Charles never felt deprived, nor did his sister Edith, born three years after him.

Walter and Mary Williams, their parents, were religious people. If the unborn soul chooses its parents for Incarnation in this world, Charles must have chosen them. Or, alternatively, it was their influence that made religion important to him from the beginning. Church-going was for him a constant delight. When only three years old he walked into church "as if he owned the place."[1] He apparently had no time of adolescent doubt or repudiation of his faith. Instead, he saw more deeply into religion as the years passed, and he was always a member of the Church of England.

For two years he attended University College, London, but, unable to afford a longer stay, he did not take a degree. Instead, he went to work in a Methodist bookshop for a short time. In 1908 he began working as a proofreader at the Oxford University Press in London and remained there, doing various types of work, for the rest of his life. He married Florence Conway in 1917, and they had one son, Michael. His love for his wife, which always had a religious dimension, is reflected especially in his early poetry. After his marriage, the chief events of his life were the publication of his writings, sometimes several of them in a year.

When World War II came, the London division of the Oxford University Press was evacuated to Oxford, and here Williams continued to write and lecture. He had given evening lectures for the Literary Institute of the London County Council. Now he was more widely in demand as a lecturer, both at the University and for various literary and professional societies. He became one of the "Inklings," an informal group of whom the most famous were J. R. R. Tolkien and C. S. Lewis, two who took religion as seriously as he did.[2] Discussions among Lewis, Williams, and Tolkien must have influenced all of their writings to some extent. In 1943 Oxford University recognized Williams's ability by giving him an honorary M.A. degree. Although the war threw its shadow on him as on others, he continued to be busy and productive until almost the day of his death. He died just after the war ended on May 15, 1945. On his tombstone in St. Cross churchyard in Oxford is inscribed, "Charles Williams, Poet . . . Under the Mercy."

In a way, his writings can be seen as a continuation of the conversation which, for most people, was the most striking aspect of his personality. When not reading or writing, Williams was talking. His friends said that whenever you had a conversation with him he made you feel, by his own vivid interest, a much more able and interesting person than you ordinarily were. His talk was always stimulating because his own insight into life, religion, and literature was so keen. The same originality of approach carries over into his writing.

The scope of his work is very wide, including biography, literary criticism, theology, and many reviews of other people's writings, as well as the drama, novels, and poetry that represent his chief contribution to English literature. His theological essays, particularly the book called *He Came Down from Heaven,* should be read along with his creative works; and, in criticism, his *Figure of Beatrice. A Study in Dante,* is especially important for ideas found in the drama, novels, and poetry.

What, then, are the exciting ideas that permeate both his life and his writings? As religion was the main force in his life, so his major creative works are religious in nature. The first recurring idea that we may mention is that of the approach to God through the Affirmative Way. This means finding God in all His works—realizing, ultimately, that He is greater than any of them—but seeing also that each "image" or created work contains something of Him. So, as Williams shows in *The Figure of Beatrice,* Dante the poet found in the girl Beatrice a "God-bearer," someone who pointed him on to seek God Himself, and so, for Williams, any person in love is very close to God, for he sees in his beloved a perfection that only God sees as well. This perfection is the truth about that person, even though that truth be dimmed or lost sight of with time and circumstances. Another God-bearing image is nature, as it was seen by the poet William Wordsworth.

The Affirmative Way, or the affirmation of images, as Williams sometimes calls it, is in contrast to the Negative Way, which, though also valid, seeks to shut out all images in order to concentrate on God. So St. Augustine used to walk with his eyes cast down, not wanting to be distracted from God by the things God had made. Both these Ways appear markedly in the Taliessin poems and in the novel, *The Place of the Lion,* though they are, of course, found elsewhere in Williams's works.

A related theme is expressed in a quotation that Williams frequently used; its source is unknown. It is, "This also is Thou. Neither is this Thou," meaning that all things contain God but no one of them encompasses or expresses Him wholly. The first sentence, "This also is Thou," means holding to the affirmation of God in everything when all seems to go wrong and God seems completely absent. We see this theme especially in the plays and in such a novel as *War in Heaven.*

Exchange, or substitution, is another of the ideas on which Williams built his life and his writings. It is closely related to the Incarnation of Jesus Christ and to His Atonement. For in the Atonement, Christ, in the form of man, substituted Himself for humanity; He bore the weight of their sins and infirmities and transformed that dreary weight into His own adequacy and energy at the time of the Resurrection. To use another expression, Christ exchanged His perfect being for man's imperfect one. Therefore, Williams reasoned, we should all follow Christ's example and in His spirit and strength, substitute ourselves, when we can, for other people who need us; we should exchange our strength for their weakness, or bear their burdens as Christ bore ours. Williams liked to quote the line from St. Mark's Gospel about Jesus at his crucifixion: "He saved others; Himself he could not save."[3] Jesus had brought healing to many, but on the Cross he seemed helpless. Williams believed we are all meant to obtain our salvation, not through our own efforts, but through other people. The idea of exchange is seen throughout his works, but is especially vivid in *Descent into Hell*.

A related theme is that of "coinherence," or living from others and constantly in relationship to them. Coinherence is a wider application of exchange; it involves our lives with those of others everywhere and in the past as well as the present—so Pauline, in *Descent into Hell*, can help her ancestor who lived four hundred years earlier. We are separate, independent beings, but if we live in coinherence we are at the same time in a loving relationship to all other created beings. We do not, in the manner of Williams's villains in the novels, pursue our proud, separate ways, regardless of other people. Like Dindrane in the poems, we pray for the world, and whether we live a secluded or an active life, we are involved with the world. Sometimes, like Lester in *All Hallows' Eve*, we might, if we are trying to live in coinherence, have a glimpse of the redeemed City, where it is the rule of life.

The City is one of Williams's most important concepts. It is more than just an idealization of the London that he knew. Like Dr. Samuel Johnson before him, Williams loved London and never wanted to live anywhere else, but as he grew older and his ideas matured, he came to see that the redeemed City, where everyone lived in coinherence, was a reality and that the imperfections so obvious to most of us are a failure in perception, a lack of realization of the harmony that is the City's nature. How else are we to understand the startling remark he made to an acquaintance who met him in the street and said, "How are you?" His answer was, "In the City and under the Mercy."[4] Of course he was not blind to evil and ugliness, but he achieved the heightened consciousness that the mystics have: the City was a reality and he lived in it. He must have known what William Blake meant when he wrote, "I am in God's presence night and day, / And he never turns his face away."[5]

Chapter Two
The Plays

Charles Williams's early drama consists of several masques written for private production at the Oxford University press and a volume entitled *Three Plays*. In all of these early plays, especially in one called *The Rite of the Passion* (from *Three Plays*), he presents ideas to be developed in his other writings. But as plays they are not consistently effective and their style is imitative and occasionally obscure. His more mature plays are the ones to be considered here.

He was a part of the church drama movement that, starting in the early years of the twentieth century, received much encouragement in the 1930s from the Bishop of Chichester, George Bell.[1] Bell believed that drama, like the other arts, has a close connection with religion. Largely due to his influence, church drama in England became important again for the first time since the Middle Ages.[2] He appointed E. Martin Browne (who later produced Williams's *Thomas Cranmer of Canterbury*) as the first diocesan Director of Drama, and he encouraged Williams along with other young playwrights such as T. S. Eliot and Christopher Fry. Martin Browne organized the Pilgrim Players, two groups of professional actors who produced religious plays in the early years of the war; Ruth Spalding's Oxford Pilgrims asked Williams for scripts and produced a number of his plays.[3]

It was for such groups and for performance in particular churches that Williams wrote his drama. He did not write for the commercial theater and probably never thought in terms of wide recognition. Yet such a play as *Thomas Cranmer* would surely hold its own on Broadway or in the West End of London just as well as T. S. Eliot's *The Cocktail Party* or Christopher Fry's *The First Born*.

Williams's plays are dominantly dramas of ideas. In the words of Anne Ridler, "They have dramatic life, they have suspense, but the excitement derives from the clash of ideas, not of persons."[4] A conflict of ideas must have gone on in Williams's mind much of the time. He had a natural skepticism and a desire always to see the other side of a question. He liked thinking in paradoxes, as is shown by such a typical comment as, "Life . . . is a good thing, and somehow unendurable."[5] Though deeply religious himself, he valued the skeptical treatment of religion in Montaigne and Voltaire,[6] and his *Descent of the Dove,* subtitled "A Short History of the Holy Spirit in the Church," is marked by a delicate irony throughout. His own passionate belief never obscured for him the fact that others believed, with some reason and justice, differently.

His faith, then, was never blind or unquestioning. Religion, he felt, thrived on questions. In his comments on the Book of Job he says that man is meant to doubt and to argue about religion: "A great curiosity ought to exist concerning divine things. Man was intended to argue with God."[7] It was, he felt, the angry, tortured Job whom God approved, not the three orthodox friends, placidly sure of all the answers; for in God's astringent remark on the folly of the comforters Williams says, "The pretence that we must not ask God what he thinks he is doing (and is therefore doing) is swept away. The Lord demands that his people shall demand an explanation from him. . . . Humility has never consisted in not asking questions."[8] He says in one of his essays that most religious plays are bad because they are too obviously propaganda. Religious plays, therefore, to Williams's mind, should stir up discussion and argument by a thoughtful treatment of real issues.[9]

Christian drama, he also believed, must "consider the nature of God,"[10] and God is the moving force behind the action of all his plays—God, who is mercy, mystery, power, infinite and demanding love. In various ways Williams expounds this theme, and one cannot say that there is "development" in the mature plays. They were all written, and some of them produced, between 1936 and 1941, a short span of time. *Thomas Cranmer of Canterbury,* produced in 1936, was markedly different from any of his earlier plays in its originality of style, the breaking away from blank verse and using a freer rhythm and internal rhyme—but the other eight plays that followed it did not surpass it, either in cogency of ideas or brilliance of style.

Different readers have their preferences, but the nine plays are all concerned with "the relation of the individual soul and God."[11] The order in which we shall now consider them is not chronological but is determined by various themes as they bear on this central relationship.

The Death of Good Fortune (1939)

This is a short play with the theme that "All luck is good"—that is, whatever happens to people, though it may seem unfortunate, disastrous, or purely evil, is actually sent from God and is capable of producing good in the recipient.

It is a Christmas play, for, although Jesus does not appear as a character, his birth has made possible a new understanding of luck. Luck can no longer be considered arbitrary (now good, now bad); God's coming into the world has shown the divine nature in everything. Love is the basic, underlying truth, though on the surface of things there may seem to be discord.

The characters, except for Mary, the mother of Jesus, are the abstractions of a morality play: Good Fortune, a charming young man; the King, to whom Good Fortune has given victory over his enemies; the Lover; the Magician; the Youth; the Old Woman, who is seeking a house of her own; and the Girl, who is skeptical about the powers of Good Fortune. Mary states the theme of the play in a speech at the beginning and brings about the apparent death of Good Fortune, who has forgotten, since the fall of man, his true heavenly nature and needs to relearn it. Mary causes him to fall down in the city square as if dead. Immediately there is consternation among the others, for the "luck" of each vanishes: the King's enemies begin to take over the country; the Old Woman loses all her savings and the house she had been promised; the Lover is deserted by his sweetheart; the Magician can no longer see into the future. The Girl, who had half believed in Good Fortune in spite of her pessimism, is grief-stricken.

The Lover, however, regains his poise, saying that even though he might lose his beloved, the glorious fact of Love does not alter. Good Fortune, he affirms, is *not* dead. The King, who cannot understand such talk, begs the Magician to help him, and the Magician has a vision of a marvellous star moving through the skies "spending its glory everywhere" (190) and finally coming to rest on earth, on Mary. He begs Mary to explain what has happened. Mary's answer is that when Good Fortune dies one must bid him rise again. She then reveals to the "dead" young man, Good Fortune, that his birth was at the birth of Christ and his real name, which he must henceforth use, is Blessed Luck. The young man, awakened, tells them what he saw during his deathlike trance and asks if they will now accept him in his new role—can they accept that all luck from now on is to be welcomed as good? The Magician, the Lover, and the Girl choose to follow the new doctrine. The King and the Old Woman, still keenly aware of their losses, refuse. Mary blesses them all and turns to the audience to remind them that they too must choose to believe the idea or not.

This play, if well acted or carefully studied, must inevitably stir up in the audience or reader the questions that Williams hoped to arouse. Is its theme accepted in orthodox Christianity? If so, are most of us very far from being Christian? Surely, we say, the Woman's loss of her property is not *good;* she is now quite destitute. Part of Williams's talent lies in his ability to bring the reader face to face with such opposing points of view. The characters are abstract but their situations are very real. The Lover and the Magician can accept the idea more easily than the others because they are less tied to material things. The Girl, too, is essentially unworldly. We ask if we, like these three, have hearts uncluttered by a desire for possessions and enlightened by a vision of God in life, so that we can understand all luck as good.

Williams brings home the theme in another way also—through the speeches of Mary, particularly at the opening of the play. Her first words are the key ones: "Incipit vita nova: substance is love, love substance" (179). *Substance* is used here and elsewhere in the play to show the solidity and firmness, the everlastingness, of Love. Love is "that which underlies phenomena; the permanent substratum of things,"[12] and its being so gives hope to a world of chance and change. Mary understands, though, that appearances can belie this truth; she sees the ambiguity in appearances—what happens does not always *look* like the action of a God who is Love. Yet "His are all the alterations: and here shall be ours" (179). By alterations she means simply changes or so-called luck. She asserts that God is in charge of all luck or changes, and here, in this "death" to be enacted on the stage, will be *our* changes—we will come to see the truth. Mary's own conviction of it has come through having suffered with and identified herself with her Son. She has been "struck by seven swords" (179) but knows now that no pain or misery can alter the glorious truth: "Since my Son died, all things are good luck, and fate and good luck and heaven are one name" (183). She remains unheard and unobserved by the others on the stage until the Magician, in his vision, sees Love itself, in the form of the great star, glide into the body of Mary (190).

Mary's gentle insistence, then, along with the dilemma of the King and the Old Woman, carries the conviction of the play. Her emphasis on choice at the end brings the main idea, that all life is good, back to the audience; they, like the characters, must choose to believe it or not.

Do most people today believe that all luck is good? Obviously not, but then most of the world is not turned to God. God, as Williams understands Him, contains within Himself all good and also what looks like evil. Evil, under God, is always capable of being recognized as good or love. Therefore, the human distinction between good and evil must not exist on God's level. The opposites that we see—good and evil, dark and light, innocence and experience—are transcended by God, and His greater synthesis can be accepted by man through faith and a developed imagination.

And yet—the reader of *The Death of Good Fortune* may want to turn away, baffled, like the King and the Old Woman. Before deciding that we cannot believe all luck to be good, let us see how Williams sets forth in his other plays a way to this essential understanding.

A first step to be taken is to accept that the meaning and purpose of life can only be found in God; in and by himself man is helpless. Paradoxically, he can achieve his full stature as a spiritual being only by seeing that as a separate individual he is nothing—he comes to his full powers not on his own but by entering into his part of God's glory.

Thomas Cranmer of Canterbury (1935)

The understanding of one's own "nothingness" is a central theme in Williams's first successful play, *Thomas Cranmer of Canterbury*, written for performance in the cloisters of Canterbury Cathedral for the summer festival in 1935.

Thomas Cranmer (1489–1556), made Archbishop of Canterbury by Henry VIII, was of a studious, gentle nature, a man of peace who was thrust by circumstances into the turmoil of the Reformation. In those days when Protestantism was just coming into being, he tried to steer a middle course between the reformers and the Catholic Church. Protected by Henry because he made possible the king's divorce from Catherine of Aragon and his marriage to Anne Boleyn, Cranmer was accused of heresy after Henry's death and burned at the stake by Queen Mary.

This story Williams tells in a stylized, poetic play that telescopes time and therefore seems to move quickly through the events leading to Cranmer's martyrdom. In the published version of the play, key dates and brief notations about his career are printed in the margins to orient the reader; in the performance, the chronology was indicated by a child sitting at the side of the stage and turning the pages of a book that set forth these incidents and dates. The dialogue on stage is interspersed with choruses by the Singers, who chant passages from the Psalms or from the Book of Common Prayer, which was written by Cranmer when he revised the liturgy of the Roman Catholic Church.

The play begins in Cambridge, where Cranmer is happy in his peaceful, scholarly life but aware of the tension between Catholics and those, like himself, who see that the Church has lost its original purity. Catholics and Protestants hurl reproaches at each other, "Adoration!" being the constant cry of the Catholics, and "Communion!" of the Protestants. In the first scene, where Cranmer hopes, in a soliloquy, that the King's law will enforce God's will, appears the most striking character in the play, the Skeleton, who hints that this wish will be granted—God's will is about to be done, through Cranmer.

At King Henry's urging, Cranmer becomes Archbishop and sanctions the king's divorce and remarriage. When Henry turns against

Anne Boleyn, Cranmer pleads for her, but to no avail; she is led away by the Skeleton. Cranmer encourages the reading of the Bible in English and incurs the wrath of both the Lords and the Commons. King Henry protects Cranmer from his enemies, and after Henry's death, the Lords who rule for Edward VI allow Cranmer to write the Book of Common Prayer.

In Part 2, the young King Edward dies and Mary comes to the throne. Cranmer is fearful, knowing that now the persecution of Protestants is beginning; and also he is troubled because he himself has sanctioned the burning of Catholics. Queen Mary demands Cranmer's recantation and when he tries to temporize he is unfrocked, and the crozier is wrenched from his hand. He is told to submit to Rome or be burned, and at last he submits. But to his surprise, the Queen orders him to be burned anyway and his recantation to be publicly proclaimed. After an agonizing exchange with the Skeleton, Cranmer realizes he is to die. He withdraws his recantation and declares that his right hand, which signed the recantation papers, will be thrust first into the fire. He is hurried away to the stake.

The life of Archbishop Cranmer, until near its end, was not outwardly dramatic; and in Williams's play the action is inner, rather than outward or obvious. It lies in a progressive unfolding of Cranmer's nature and motives. As Williams portrays him, he is weak and vacillating, fearful of pain and death, essentially a good man—a peacemaker, a scholar, a man of prayer—but not a hero. He tries to be honest but does not understand himself. Beneath his concern for King Henry, his tenderness for Anne, and his worry over having a part in religious persecution, there lies a deep-rooted self-love. By the end of the play, however, he has been stripped of all intellectual and spiritual pretensions. Just before his death he finds something better than his personal being, for he turns away from self and flees into God's love.

He is brought to this saving knowledge of his own powerlessness by the Skeleton, the enigmatic character who so puzzled the first reviewers of the play. What does he represent? At times he seems to be only a sprightly personification of Death (he puts his cloak over Anne and takes her out to die; he tells Cranmer he will catch him in the end). In the original production the Skeleton wore black tights, a black cloak lined with green, and a mask that hid his eyes—so Death might be dressed. But his wry or sarcastic comments on the action, heard usually by only the audience, suggest a more complex personality.

Early in the play he comments that heaven gives everyone his desire; let a man beware of what he asks for—he might be sorry after he gets it. When King Henry complains to Cranmer "Thomas, Thomas, Anne is not what I thought," the Skeleton looks at the audience and says, "A remark few of you die without making" (13). When Cranmer rebukes the aggrieved Commons, who want a return to mystery in religion, the Skeleton points out that he is too positive in his opinions, saying, "You speak well, Thomas, but you do not know all. / No man ever refused adoration yet, / but in it was something which was death to refuse" (29). Whether jokingly satirical or serious in his remarks, the Skeleton seems always to plead for a truth that includes some element of both sides. Swift and agile, he runs and leaps about the stage, showing now one point of view and now another—or showing that they are part of the same point. When the conflicting, tumultuous voices cry, "Adoration" or "Communion," "Up with the clergy," or "Down with the clergy," and hurl "Antichrist" at each other, the Skeleton takes the form of a blind beggar, calling out, "O my people, where is the way? / Do you hear me, zealots? Where is the way?" (12) and a little later, "I am the way, / I the division, the derision, where / the bones dance in the darkening air" (12).

There are other suggestions that the Skeleton, for all his sinister aspect, is a presentation of the view not of either side but of the God that both sides claim. At his first appearance, the Singers chant, "Blessed is he that cometh in the name of the Lord" (5).[13] When King Henry warns Cranmer that publishing the Bible in English will bring trouble upon him, the Skeleton says, in the words of Christ, "My hour is not yet come"[14] and then, "but I will show / a little prelude of the hour of you and me" (20) and proceeds to allow the Lords and Commons to raise a commotion about Cranmer, urging that he be sent to the Tower. The Skeleton says he was "born under Virgo" (34),[15] prophesies that he will call Cranmer, as Christ called his Apostles, "no more servant now, but friend" (35).[16] And as Cranmer's friend he uses again the words of Christ, "You believe in God; believe also in me" (35). [17]

The Skeleton suggests Christ or God also in the way that he sees into the future; he knows and declares Cranmer's fate and the fate of everyone. In the very first scene, Cranmer, disturbed by the opposing factions of priest and preacher, speaks of his longing for God's will to be done through the King. If this could be, he, Cranmer, would willingly suffer. He little knows that heaven will take him at his word; Henry will, by making him Archbishop, cause him to be outcast, martyred. But the Skeleton knows it. He knows, too, Cranmer's passion for justice, his attempt to get fair treatment for Anne Boleyn without disloyalty to Henry.

In the moving last scene of Part One, the Skeleton confronts Cranmer openly. He has tried, up to now, to suggest to Cranmer's mind that he is too positive; and Cranmer has felt disturbed and stumbled a bit in his speech. But he recovers his self-confidence as he speaks of his Book of Common Prayer. As he reads out parts of it, the Skeleton makes telling comments. At the sentence beginning "It is very meet, right, and our bounden duty, that we should at all times and in all places, give thanks," he says,

> "Ah, how the sweet words ring their beauty.
> *it is meet, right, and our bounden duty,*
> but will you sing it with unchanged faces
> when God shall change the times and the places?" (32)

Here the audience begins to see that the Skeleton is speaking the same doctrine as that of Mary in *The Death of Good Fortune*—no matter what the luck, the change of time or place, the Christian is to give thanks. The Skeleton's astringent personality is somehow a glimpse of the quality of Christ's love. As Cranmer continues writing about being "a reasonable, holy, and lively sacrifice" to God, the Skeleton warns that it is a pity if people don't see what the words really mean. How, we wonder, will Cranmer stand up to being a sacrifice? Will he be able to give thanks then? Will God be in the burning as he is in the beautiful words of the prayers? The Skeleton says God will be, for God is in all things.

He tries to convince Cranmer of God's inclusiveness as the scene ends, by making himself known. Cranmer cannot see very well; his eyes are weak (a suggestion that he cannot yet see Christ in His multiple roles). But he asks courteously, "Friend do I know you? / Are you of my household?" (34). The Skeleton answers, "An in-dweller, my Lord," and presently he adds, "I am the delator of all things to their truth" (34). Cranmer is afraid and begins to pray, "God, without whom nothing is strong," but the Skeleton inter-rupts, "I respected you, Thomas; I heard; I am here. / Do not fear; I am the nothing you meant" (35). Profoundly frightened, Cranmer cries, "Christ or devil, leave me to lie in peace," to which the Skeleton replies in words that show the immense vitality of God's love, "If I leave you to peace I shall leave you to lie, / to change without changing, to live without living" (35). Cranmer must be made to see that God is a living, uncomfortable presence, a tre-mendous love that will cut through pain and difficulty to a greater life beyond. The love is made even more evident in his next speech, after Cranmer, in desperation at sensing a force he cannot under-stand, calls out, "God, God, stop the world moving!" and the Skeleton answers,

> "Stop me loving, would you? Stop me proving
> the perfect end in the diagram of bones?
> You believe in God; believe also in me;
> I am the Judas who betrays men to God.
> Friend, friend!" (35)

Not until he is near his death does Cranmer begin to see the truth about himself. The Skeleton, "delator of all things to their truth," shows how each conviction must contain knowledge of its opposite and something of God in both. When Cranmer accepts the Arch-bishopric he realizes that in times before he has, for the sake of a quiet life, been unwilling to act on his beliefs. The Skeleton shows him that the scholarly life, which he always thought of as more noble than other things men desire, is, like Anne's wish to be a queen and the Lords' wish for wealth, only an "image," something legitimate enough but less than God. Again, he has always sought honesty, but does not fully believe all that he writes in the Prayer

Book. Then, dreadfully, he comes to see that he has no courage. He recants and agrees to submit to the Pope because he is afraid, feeling "utterly lost and damned" (51). But he is to feel even worse when, having denied his principles to save his life, he finds that he is doomed anyway. His is the misery of self-reproach: "They will burn me; I know it; I denied God for naught" (53).

At this dark moment the Skeleton gives him a glimpse of truth, telling him that he will see Christ, but he must "see his back first— I am his back" (54). Cranmer begins to understand, for he says, "Can life itself be redemption? all grace but grace? / all this terror the agonizing glory of grace?" (54). Here again are the opposites— terror is somehow glory; they are one and the same. The Skeleton, as Christ's back, is the necessary suffering and negation to be accepted as a condition of seeing Christ's face. Man must see himself as "nothing" on his own; all his achievement comes from the grace of God. This Cranmer begins to understand, but he cannot help, being human, trying to achieve some merit on his own: he will thrust his hand, that signed the recantation papers, into the fire first. The relentless Skeleton shows him that even in this noble gesture of self-sacrifice there is pride; even the martyrdom is not purely unselfish, because it is the only course left to him. He forces Cranmer at last to admit that he is truly "nothing" on his own. Before his physical death he dies to self, sacrificing the last vestige of self-esteem when he admits, "If the Pope had bid me live, I should have served him" (59).

E. Martin Browne, who played the Skeleton in the first production, calls the Skeleton "a symbol of the Necessary Love which compels the Christian, as it first compelled his Master, to find God, who is eternal life, through the gate of death."[18] What seems evil is, for the believer, a necessary path to ultimate perfection. He must go down before he can rise. The gate of death does not mean physical death only—it is any suffering or diminishing. These "evils" are actually good because God is in them, or, as the Skeleton shows, God *is* the evil, which is the other side, or back, of good.

The play is full of conflicts. The central one, that of Cranmer against the Skeleton (his small, personal self against his Christ self), has been indicated. Cranmer accepts the nothingness of the small finite self and in so doing is redeemed. His conflict with royal authority—with King Henry, who brings him into public life, and more painfully with Queen Mary—ends in his submission, but it is only a kind of exterior manifestation of his inner conflict with the Skeleton. His triumph is not in his decision to withdraw his recantation but in his last confession that in his own strength alone he could only have chosen the absence of pain.

There is also the conflict between Catholics and Protestants, and there is the massed force of both the Lords and the Commons arrayed now and then against Cranmer; his honesty and simplicity offend the greedy Lords, interested only in getting for themselves the wealth of the Catholic Church; and his sweet reasonableness annoys both the superstitious Commons and the extremists who want to root all papists out of the land. Williams shows us Cranmer's era as one of danger, violence, tumult, and strife, where no person or cause is safe. Yet within this turbulence, undergirding it, is the beauty and stability of the Kingdom of God: the sweet voices of the Singers, chanting Psalms or passages from the Book of Common Prayer, contrast strongly with the brawling voices of the mobs, the sharp, unpitying voice of Queen Mary, Cranmer's agonizing cries at the end, and the Skeleton's clear, steady answers. The play is a symphony of blending and contrasting voices.

It is short, with an acting time of only an hour and a half, yet it touches on all the major events of Cranmer's career. Its swiftness is emphasized by the frequent appearance of the verb *run*. Not only does the Skeleton run and leap about on the stage, but his energy and vitality are stressed by his often speaking of speed or running. To Cranmer, unwilling to "see" him, the Skeleton says, "Do you run to me or do I run to you?" (35). Near the end, Cranmer prays, "What shall I then? despair? thou art not despair. / Into thee now do I run, into thy love" (57). His running into God's love is in the mind of the audience at the very end, when only the burning is left to be done, and the Skeleton's urgent word, "Speed!" is echoed by Cranmer and everyone present as they all hurry out.

From the first production of *Cranmer,* Williams's use of a chorus was probably attributed to the influence of T. S. Eliot, whose *Murder in the Cathedral* had been produced for the Canterbury Festival just

a year earlier. We do not know whether Williams consciously imitated Eliot. Later, speaking to an audience that had just seen *Seed
of Adam* he said, "Mr. Eliot has made choruses a little difficult. I
know all about the Greeks, but they do not prevent one being told
one is copying Mr. Eliot."[19]

Eliot's chorus is the most important part of his play, creating its
atmosphere and accounting for its poetic excellence. In *Cranmer* the
Singers are less a part of the action. Their chanted words, such as
"O Lord God of my salvation, I have cried / day and night before
thee:" (49) undoubtedly express Cranmer's feelings, but the voices
are more remote and formal than those of the Women of Canterbury
in Eliot's play. Always Williams's Singers are more detached, almost
impersonal, giving expression to universal emotions and eternal
truths.

The House of the Octopus (1945)

The chief idea of *Cranmer*, the need to see one's own personal
nothingness, is again a theme in *The House of the Octopus*, a play with
a twentieth-century setting. Here the spirit of God, who brings a
man to see his sin of self-sufficiency, is called the Flame. Williams
describes this character in a note to the first edition of the play as
representing "that energy which went to the creation and was at
Pentecost (as it were) re-delivered in the manner of its own august
covenant to the Christian Church." He suggests that the person
taking the part wear a flame-colored costume with an outer cloak
of "a deep star-sprinkled blue": "When he speaks to the Christians
he throws back his outer cloak; when to the others, he gathers it
round him" (246–47). The Flame serves somewhat the same purpose
as the Skeleton in *Cranmer*, presenting another aspect of the action
and also taking part in it.

On an island in "the outer seas" a new Christian Church is threatened by the pagan empire of P'o-lu which, like an octopus, stretches
its tentacles and catches all the islands. A plot by Assantu, the son
of a sorcerer, and his wife, who hates Christians, delivers the missionary priest, Anthony, into the hands of his enemies from P'o-lu.

Anthony's flock have to submit to an examination by the officers
of P'o-lu. One of them, Alayu, fearful of pain, denies she is a

Christian, but she is killed anyway. A superior officer decides that the others are not to be killed but brainwashed so that they can be integrated with the pagans. He begins to corrupt Anthony by suggesting to him that P'o-lu and Christianity are not very different after all—the apparent discrepancies are merely a matter of words used in different senses. Anthony, not realizing his own selfishness, desires to gain more souls for Christ and wonders if he might lose some by a profitless debate over mere words. To his surprise, his parishioners see his doubts about words as a faithless compromise with the enemy; they will have none of it. Nor will they agree with him that Alayu was an apostate; they know her devotion to Christ was real, even though, in fear, she denied Him.

At this crisis in Anthony's leadership, one of the young Christians says, "Let the Spirit judge between us," and the Flame immediately appears and persuades them all to speak the real truth. Under this compulsion Anthony confesses that he wants his followers to look to him as God. He says he wants to be "their father, their centre, almost their creator" (297). Relentlessly, the Flame asks Assantu to interpret this speech of Anthony's, and its ugly truth comes forth in an image of eating; for, throughout the play, eating or being eaten is a reference to the Eucharist, either true or twisted. Anthony strayed from the true way of Christ when he said according to Assantu's interpretation: "I wish not to be eaten, but to eat others; / I wish to grow great and thrive on others:" (298). Further, Anthony's real meaning as interpreted by the sorcerer is that the priest's fatherly, personal power was damaged by Alayu's denial of Christianity.

Assantu says that Anthony is saying to the dead girl: "I must have you for my own, wholly my own, none / shall have you but I. I am the Father, and hungry" (300). At this interpretation of his words, Anthony, horrified, begins to see the depth of his own sin— he had covered over his real motives with plausible, "good" language. The ghost of Alayu appears to Anthony to ask him to forgive her for being afraid. She says she had mistaken human love for the love of God. She wants to make restitution, and the Flame, who stands "between the charity of the living and the dead," (309) asks her to bear the burden of Anthony's fear of death, which will soon be upon him. She, who had been so fearful for herself, agrees now to "carry" Anthony's dread, and Anthony humbles himself to owe her a debt of gratitude. Now he can die purposefully as she was unable to do. Anthony is taken by the officer to be given as food for the octopus; the other Christians (save one, who is spared to take the Gospel to others) are killed by machine-gun fire.

In this play, as in *Cranmer*, Williams presents the story of apparent failure—Christians overcome by a harsh, opposing force and losing their lives. But in both plays the inner drama is all-important; what seems outwardly like failure is the triumph of spirit, brought about in both plays by the characters' realization of their own weakness. Anthony, as the founder of the mission on the faraway island, has been so loved and revered by his flock that he thinks of himself as indispensable for the young Church. It seems something *he* has created, whereas he should be only a vehicle for the spirit of God. After the Flame has shown him the horrible truth, Anthony finally understands that he is nothing on his own; he must live wholly from God.

The same need to give up one's own desires and be humble before God is seen in Alayu. She has mistaken her pleasure in love and in the loving companionship of her fellow Christians, for the spirit of God within her. When the pleasure is withdrawn and she is asked to suffer, her fear of pain overcomes her faith. Only after death does she realize her fault and learn true humility.

The idea of self-naughting applies not only to individuals but also to the Church. Williams's concern in this play with the corporate Body of Christ is seen in the importance of the Flame, the austere, selfless power which is God's spirit. The Flame's activity is to save the young innocent Church from the power of P'o-lu; but as great an enemy as the pagan empire is the self-sufficiency that can be felt by a group as well as by one person. Anthony sees this danger to the Church after his own enlightenment.

The great example for the Church, he sees, is in the complete "naughting" of Himself by Christ, its origin. In accepting His suffering and death, Christ gave up His own will completely, and His sacrifice of all ego demands is celebrated by Christians in the Eucharist. Anthony, just before he surrenders to the Marshall of P'o-lu, speaks for himself and his Church: "if Christ must actualize himself in our death / it is we whom first he actualized in his own, / and still in his Eucharist" (319). Throughout the play, a contrast is drawn between the God of the Christians, who gives himself to his people, even to the point of being eaten, and P'o-lu, who is always referred to as the "hungry Father" and demands constant human sacrifices for his food. And as already seen, one indication of Anthony's sin is his inner identification with the wrathful "Father" who consumes his people in a place of decay and "everlasting eating" (300).

At the opposite extreme from Anthony's self-naughting is the pitiful character Assantu, who is only nominally a Christian and has some supernatural powers that he uses for his own ends. He kills his wife's brother in order to betray Anthony to the soldiers, and he ends by going mad and believing himself to be the cannibalistic "Father" who can only live by torture and death.

The Flame is by far the most interesting character in the play. He appears suddenly and silently whenever anyone mentions the Holy Spirit or prayer. Like the Skeleton in *Cranmer,* his words are usually unheard except by the audience, but he is the moving power of the action. He first repulses Assantu, the false Christian, but his main business is to protect the young Church; to this end he purges the souls of Anthony and Alayu of pride and fear; and at the end, after the Christians have been killed by the guns, he shows them that they are now in heaven, saying, "Rise, holy ones; rise, confessors and martyrs! / saints, arise! all is done; I am here" (323).

Like the Skeleton, the Flame now and then makes ironic comments. The Christians, urging Anthony to seek safety, ask him, "Do you doubt, father / that you leave us, everywhere and always, with / God Almighty?" and the Flame observes, "And they say his fatherhood is more efficient than yours" (261). Again, as Anthony is trying to decide whether to compromise with P'o-lu, he prays for guidance, saying, "Blessed Spirit, show me what I should do." The Flame says pointedly, "Indeed . . . but most prayer is instruction to him" (286).

The Flame makes the audience vividly aware of the invisible world existing right beside the visible and tangible. And in the redemption of Anthony and Alayu he shows the reality of spiritual power. The

Flame also introduces a theme that is central in all of Williams's work—that of exchange. Williams believed that Christians are meant to bear, in a literal manner, one another's burdens, since Christ carries all our burdens and sins. Therefore, the Flame asks Alayu to carry Anthony's fear in order to redeem her sin and be a part of Christ's redemption. Alayu agrees to be afraid again, though she still is shrinking a bit. Anthony asks, "I am to owe her my own salvation from apostasy?" (309–10), and understanding that this may be, he agrees. He has at last learned to give up his idea of himself, to find his true self.

Judgement at Chelmsford (1939)

Williams's concern with the Church as an entity capable, like the individual, of both good and evil, is evident again in *Judgement at Chelmsford,* a pageant play written for the celebration of the twenty-fifth anniversary of the diocese of Chelmsford in Essex.[20] Formal in structure, it has a Prologue and Epilogue and eight separate episodes, each one portraying a scene in the history of the diocese. In the synopsis that Williams wrote to accompany the play, he explains that each episode has two aspects, the historical and the spiritual, and that in this way "the complete pageant offers a representation not only of the history of the diocese, but of the movement of the soul of man in its journey from the things of this world to the heavenly city of Almighty God" (63).

In the Prologue, the female figure of Chelmsford comes on her birthday to the gate of heaven to talk with the great Sees of Christendom—Canterbury, Jerusalem, Antioch, Rome, and Constantinople. She is stopped by the Accuser, who tells her that she cannot easily get into heaven; she must justify herself. When she asks who he is, he replies in a paraphrase of Satan's words in the Book of Job, that he has come "from going with time up and down the earth" (72) and that he was created by Primal Wisdom, Justice, and Love. He is like the Skeleton in *Cranmer* and the Flame in *The House of the Octopus,* a figure standing outside the main action but making trenchant comments on it, and, at times, moving the action in one way or another. The Accuser's function here is to make Chelmsford examine herself—is she really what she things she is? Like a devil's advocate, he insists that she look at all the "shady" incidents in her past and judge herself in the light of Love's demands.

To carry out this judgement, the Accuser shows her "how far and with what energy she has followed God" (63), and the episodes may be taken as fairly typical of the whole Church in Britain, though their immediate setting is in Essex. They begin with a scene in a modern church, where the parishioners talk over means of attracting young people to the services; their silly, futile discussion is completely irrelevant to the lives of a girl who wants to get a job in the factory and her young man, an agricultural worker—they want more "life," and cannot find it in sermons, hymns, and self-denial.

The episodes then move backward in time, for the play is anti-chronological; it starts with the present and goes backward to the climax (or time's source) of Christ's Cross. There is first a lurid scene of witch-hunting, sanctioned by the good people of the diocese; then we see the martyrdom of both a Catholic and a Protestant during the Reformation. In a painful scene of John Ball and the Peasants' Revolt, the Accuser comments bitterly on how the poor, in spite of protestations by the Church, are always driven back "down the old ways / by the wall of gold, iron and steel" (121). We see next the martyrdom of St. Osyth, the nun who was killed by invading Danes. The last scenes are less grim. Constantius of Rome visits Colchester, where he meets Helena, the daughter of King Cole, and they fall in love; from their union will come Constantine, who united Rome and the Christian Church.

From all these scenes Chelmsford has come at last to value penitence; she sees the grievous flaws in her past and realizes that she is, in herself, totally devoid of virtue. She must accept the Cross of Christ; like Cramer and Anthony, she must know her own "nothingness." As soon as she accepts the Cross, the Accuser is no longer her stern judge but her lover. He made her face the facts about herself but did so out of love, for he is "God's true knowledge of all things made" (147).

Looking at the play as a depiction of the soul's journey to God, we see the early scenes of witch-hunting as images of Hell, with the soul of man intent on gain through the selfish exploitation of others' fears. Likewise, the Reformation scenes show the soul insisting on its own "right"; it is self-centered and blind. In the episode of the hungry peasants the soul is content with its own good, heedless of the needs of others.

In the scene of the martyrdom of St. Osyth the Accuser says that it is he who shows the blessed martyrs to Chelmsford. He tells her, "The more you know me, sweet, the more you know them" (127). In other words, judgement, represented by the Accuser, always implies penitence, and with penitence comes a greater knowledge of God and the people of God. The soul is now beginning to know itself and acknowledge its own failings. Heaven is attained when the soul finds the Cross within. When it accepts, as Chelmsford does, its own nothingness and realizes its complete dependence upon God, it is lifted up to Heaven.

The action of this pageant play is in scenes involving groups of people, and the dramatic effect comes from light, color, sound, and movement on the stage. Chelmsford and the other Sees, together with the Accuser, watch the pageant and interpret it.

As the Sees come together in the Prologue and the Accuser proposes to bring Chelmsford to judgement, sounds of airplanes and bombing suggest the violence about to be exposed and the terror associated with self-revelation. Episode one opens with the noise and clamor of factories, and there is a laborers' dance that is swallowed up in a stiffer, more mechanical dance of the machine workers.

Dance movement is again effective in the witches' scene, where a fire throws a green light over everything. When Hopkins, the witch-finder, breaks up their ceremony, he forces them to run about constantly, without rest, while the terrible fiery light according to the stage instructions "glows everywhere" (91). There is violence also in the scene where a Catholic tries to snatch a Bible from a Protestant, and their struggle becomes "a whirling belligerent dance" (95).

Other effective crowd scenes show the throng of rebel poor being met by a wall of armed men; and the nuns fleeing at the time of St. Osyth's murder by the Danes. In nearly every scene a chorus, like the ones in Greek drama, explains and enlightens, or sings in hope, grief, or penitence.

The play has many affirmations, such as one by St. Osyth about her vision of the City, beginning, "I saw the City where Love loves and is loved" (126). The City, one of Williams's favorite images, is the place where no person or institution will try to dominate others, where nobody will feel his own righteousness, but where all will be a part of Christ's glory, a vast web of interrelationships having a mathematically precise beauty. Here everyone will live a rich, creative life from the Creator and will practice exchange, as do Anthony and Alayu in *The House of the Octopus;* and here all luck will be seen to be good. Acknowledging one's own nothingness, then, is not an end in itself, but a preliminary to becoming part of the glory.

Seed of Adam (1936)

In the nativity play, *Seed of Adam,* a main character, Mary, like St. Osyth in *Chelmsford,* has already become part of the glory. When Mary appears as the daughter of Adam and Eve and is betrothed to Joseph, she is remarkable for an inward ability, peace, and joy.

The play is short and deceptively simple; its sparse action contains a depth of thought and feeling to which only poetry could do justice. At the beginning, Adam, representing all mankind, appears with Eve and two of the Magi. Adam longs to return to Paradise, and he sees that others, too, are lost, beguiling the tedium of their exile in various ways. Two of the ways are represented by the two Magi: the Tsar of Caucasia and his followers symbolize a concern with outward activity, such as trade and exploration; the other, who is the Sultan of Baghdad, shows an equally hopeless absorption in the world of intellect. Both activity and intellect are poor substitutes for Paradise. But in the purity of his daughter Mary, Adam sees a chance of return to Paradise. She must marry Joseph, a young soldier in the train of the Sultan. When Eve asks why they should marry, Adam replies "Lest I should die" (155).

Mary and Joseph, alone, talk about the nature of love, and while they are speaking, the angel Gabriel appears, puts Joseph to sleep, and offers to Mary the Incarnation. They go to Bethlehem. At this point Adam returns as Augustus Caesar (for Williams has overruled time and space, and all the action is in Eternity linked with Time).

Still hoping to find someone who will show him how to return to Paradise, Adam orders a census of all mankind. But no savior comes. Instead, the Third King appears, representing, in Williams's words, "the experience of man when man thinks he has gone beyond all hope of restoration to joy" (174). He is accompanied by a Negress carrying a scythe; she represents Hell. Together they intend to destroy all mankind, and the Negress begins by advancing toward Mary, who, entirely unafraid, says, "Dearest, you will find me very indigestible" (168). And suddenly the birth of Christ is about to occur. Hell shrieks, "and holy is his Name" (169) and faints at Mary's feet. Joseph takes Mary into the stable and returns almost immediately to ask Adam to send a midwife. The Third King tells the Negress to go, saying, "deliver her and she shall deliver you" (170). She goes with Joseph, who presently comes again to tell Adam that the child has been born. All persons present and the choruses sing praises to the Christ.

An analysis of *Seed of Adam* must begin with Williams's own statement in the synopsis of the play that he wrote for the program notes. He says, "This nativity is not so much a presentation of the historic facts as of their spiritual value. The persons of the play, besides being dramatic characters, stand for some capacity or activity of man" (173).

The need for the birth of Christ is made vivid by the situation of man at the start of the play. The Tsar and the semi-chorus who follows him feel the attraction of the outer world, but their efforts are tedious and pointless.

Likewise, the Sultan's offer of intellectual pleasures—"gnomic patterns of diagrammatic thrills" (152)—seems only a poor substitute of "golden chatter" for the "golden matter" (152) of the Tsar. The semi-chorus who follow the Sultan, like those in the Tsar's train, know that in truth they have nothing; they are all descendants of Adam, shut out from the real joy of Paradise. Having given up hope of returning there, they occupy themselves with diversions for which Adam rebukes them. He assures them that if they found Paradise they would find everything, but they cannot see how to find it—"What is this way?" asks one, "behind what sight or sound?" (153). They cannot conceive of something that is inaccessible to the senses. So Williams pictures men in all ages, drifting, wistfully longing for a fulfillment they cannot find. They chatter and fight and "run about like monkeys," (stage direction) and Adam says sadly to Eve, "They have not the pain that in us stops us fighting" (154).

Why is Adam more aware than the chorus of the loss of Paradise? Perhaps because it was he who lost it. He represents the capacity of man to see more than the present situation. In Paradise it was Adam and Eve who determined to know evil as well as good. Now Adam is sure there is more to life than the external occupations and mental or imaginative pursuits. He cannot understand, though, that Paradise can be within a person, and he is puzzled by Mary, who seems always so happy and unaware of any lack. He contrasts her with himself, "My want / worries at my throat, while she wants nothing, / nor ever sighs for nor even denies Paradise" (155–56). Eve replies perceptively, "Paradise perhaps is hers and here" (156), but Adam cannot understand this remark. He is sure, however, that Mary must not become like the "apes" of the chorus, and to remove her from their influence he asks her and Joseph to marry: "I am determined you two shall be married. / A heart of purity and a mind of justice / to be integrity" (156).

What Adam is searching for Mary has already found. Her universal goodwill reflects the all-encompassing love of God, even before the angel Gabriel comes to her. Williams implies, in fact, that the angel appears because she is ready. She represents man's intuitive knowledge of God's love, peace, and joy; and it is this openness to spiritual truth that makes possible the birth of Christ—in Bethlehem in history, and in the soul at all times.

The opposing forces in the play, then, are those that seek and find the new life, the way of return to Paradise—Adam and Eve, Mary and Joseph; and those that oppose the return, the Third King and his grim companion, the Negress who stands for Hell.

The Third King, like the Accuser, the Skeleton, and the Flame, is a paradoxical figure; they are all figures of contradiction or pain and yet, at the same time, messengers of God. The Third King represents a view of life that Adam and Eve obtained at the Fall. As Williams explains it in one of his essays, "the Adam" (i.e.,

Adam and Eve), at the creation knew only good, but they were aware that God had another knowledge, of something else, and this they also desired. Since all that God had made was good, they could not, in reality, ever know evil; but they could, and did, know good as something else—as evil. What was really good now seemed, after the Fall, like evil. Sex, for example, which had been a delight, now became something shameful. Whereas God could know evil intellectually, without partaking of it, the Adam had to experience it in their human manner, through suffering.[21] What they experienced was not just the life of toil mentioned in the Book of Genesis, but a seeing of life as completely physical and material and therefore doomed to die.

It is logical, therefore, that Williams should choose the Third King, the one who bore myrrh as a gift to the Holy Child, as his symbol of man's hopelessness. Myrrh, the bitter gum used in embalming, is a reminder of death. The Third King is the cynical voice we all have heard, saying, "No matter what you achieve in life, it all ends in death."

And yet the Third King also represents the way of Return to Paradise. Here Williams uses a striking image—the core of the apple. The apple, or fruit eaten in Paradise, he sees as pleasant at first, fragrant and delicious to the senses; when the choice to know good as evil is first made, there is a sense of exhilaration. But the core is less pleasant—if the Adam's choice is persisted in, physical life becomes dominant and evil becomes boring, "the despair of life itself prolonged through the going-on of life itself."[22] In the play, the Third King says to Adam that he was in the core of the apple which Adam threw away. He explains why the core of the fruit is the way of Return. Just as he was at the heart of the fruit, at his own heart was a worm, Hell, whom he calls "my little mother Myrrh" (165). This horrible little mother continually kills and eats the King, who is then restored, only to be eaten again. In other words, Hell feeds constantly on the false view of life that sees good *as* evil. It is then, properly speaking, Hell as well as the Third King who makes possible the way of Return. Evil, like good, is the seed of Adam.

Delivery from Hell cannot be by physical means. When Adam orders the soldiers to seize the Negress and they rush at her, she merely laughs and they fall back on their knees. Joseph draws his scimitar but falls to the ground when only touched by the Third King. The King's question "Are you come out with swords and staves to take us?" (166) with its reminder of Gethsemane,[23] emphasizes the spiritual nature of the conflict. It is only Mary, who lives in God, who can confront the Negress with the truth. She knows that Hell is powerless in the end to touch goodness; she says,

> "The stomach of the everlasting worm
> is not omnivorous; it is a poor weak thing:
> nor does the fire of Gehenna do more than redden
> the pure asbestos of the holy children. . . ." (168)

Not only is the Negress unable to harm Mary. Since all the powers of so-called evil are under the control of God, she is brought to acknowledge His dominion. More, she is the midwife who delivers the Child. In this astonishing but logical twist to the Bethlehem story, Williams again shows his conviction that "evil," Hell itself, is always doing the work of God. He sees that "rejection and destruction, as well as affirmation and creation, are instruments of the Supreme Wisdom, Power and Love."[24]

The birth of Christ is seen as putting a stop to the sin, or "hunger," that was a part of the original creation, before Adam and Eve were in the garden. Hell's "hunger" is now transmuted—she goes into the stable to devour Mary and ends by bringing forth the means to change this appetite into the perpetual self-sacrifice of Love. As in *The House of the Octopus,* the Christian God's giving of Himself is shown in contrast to a hellish need (in a god or man) to devour.

In her encounter with Hell at the climax of the play, Mary is remarkable not only for her complete absence of fear but also for her tenderness. Addressing Hell as "Dearest," she retreats from her, and as Hell advances she taunts her gently, "Sister, how slowly you carve your meat!" (168). Mary is capable of God-like, impartial love because she has given up the personal desires of a selfish human being and become a transparency for Love itself.

The House by the Stable (1939)

For Williams, as we have seen, the true Christian believes all luck to be good, and he accepts his own nothingness, realizing that he is significant, not in and of himself, but as part of the "glory." How can this insight be made practical in daily life? The answer is given in the four plays now to be analyzed.

The first of these, *The House by the Stable,* is another nativity play. The scene is Man's house (or earth) on one side of the stage and a stable on the other. The action begins with Man and Pride discussing their mutual love. Her brother, Hell, wants to trick Man at dice and win his "jewel"—his soul. Gabriel, Man's servant, announces that two poor people have come seeking shelter, and the woman is pregnant. Pride will not allow Man to have the strangers in the house, but in pity for them he lets Gabriel lodge them in the stable. As the dice game is played, Man is called for persistently by Gabriel, Joseph, and Mary, but Pride and Hell persuade him there is no sound but the wind. At last Man is sure he hears and calls for Gabriel to inquire about Mary. But when Gabriel arrives, Man is so drunk on wine that he falls asleep. Gabriel finishes the game, discovers that Pride and Hell have been cheating, and drives them away. When Man awakes, Gabriel takes him to see Mary, Joseph, and the Child; and Man, contrite about his poor offer of only a stable, takes from his breast his jewel to give to the Child Jesus.

In this simple allegory Williams has given the root cause of man's original alienation from God. It is pride that makes him feel self-sufficient and almost shuts out any vision of heavenly glory. Pride is seductive, flattering, gently insistent that Man, for love of her, shut himself away from his friends to think about his own glory. Man is so carried away by her adulation that he feels he owns the earth and is responsible to nobody. He is impatient with Gabriel's mention of God; as for the jewel, his Soul, he says, "I never found it anywhere. . . . It must needs be some old hidaway rubbish" (205). Only when he sees the holy Child does he remember that the jewel hangs around his neck. He hands it to Mary for the Child, saying humbly, "There; it was once bright; it might serve / I do not know what it is at all" (215).

As in the other plays, there is here a clear confrontation of the forces of light and darkness. The dice game, the drunken laughter and lovemaking of Man and Pride symbolize the trivia that engross the individual who has not found his center—trivia comparable to the temporary diversions of the Tsar's and the Sultan's followers in *Seed of Adam*. But even while Man encourages Pride and Hell, he is looked after by Gabriel, who takes the form of his servant and seems someone that Man has always known—perhaps symbolizing his innate awareness of God. At the climax of the play Man, engrossed in the dice game, yet keeps hearing voices, something outside himself; and when he finally rouses himself and calls for Gabriel to explain the voices, he is delivered from the clutches of Pride and Hell.

Hell is shown as a great loutish person, not so quick and bright as his sister but more sinister. He wants Man to come to his "house," which can best be found through Pride. Hell is no match for Gabriel. In the lively scene where Gabriel finishes the dice game after Man has fallen asleep, the angel's majestic presence and command quickly reduce Hell and Pride to cowering and snivelling. He knocks their heads together, reveals the cheating, and makes Pride kneel and say after him, "Glory to God in the highest and on earth peace: goodwill to men." He sends Hell away saying that he could not exist at all except by divine permission: "Get to your house and the burning you made—and not even / that is your own; the fire is borrowed from heaven" (212).

Grab and Grace, or It's the Second Step (1941)

As a continuation of the story of Man, Pride, and Hell, *Grab and Grace* is even more lively and quick-moving than *The House by the Stable*. Now Pride and Hell, after a hundred years of wandering in "the malignant lands" (219), find themselves back at Man's house and decide to try again to lure him to destruction. From a bag of Hell's relics, which include such gruesome objects as a bit of Abel's blood and a piece of Adam's tooth, they pull out a rough-looking monastic garment that becomes Pride's new attire—she has heard that Man has become religious, so she will take a new name and be called Self-Respect. But Man, though he welcomes the two again, now has new friends; in addition to the servant Gabriel, his house-hold includes a stylish-looking young woman called Faith and a boy named Grace.

Man tries to persuade Faith and Pride to become friends, but Faith refuses. Hell tries to drown Grace, and while Man and Gabriel go to rescue him, Hell returns, and he and Pride seize Faith and tie her up. They shove her into the relic bag, having first emptied out its contents, and tell Man she has gone into the house. Pride, with her seductive ways, almost brings Man to love her as before, when they are interrupted by Grace, who has returned and is playing a tune on a dulcimer. Grace urges Man to listen to the music and rolls out the bag for him to sit on. While everyone's attention is focused on the bag, a knife appears through it as Faith begins to cut her way out. Free, she grapples with Pride, who has snatched a dagger from Hell's belt, and easily overcomes her. Man, mean-while, has wrestled with Hell and downed him. Grace says that Man must now decide what to do with the culprits, and reluctantly (for he loved Pride) he sends them away.

The title of this play is perfect. "Grab" suggests the slapstick quality of some of its humor, and "Grace," besides being one of the characters, indicates God's loving concern for erring Man, as it is seen at the climax of the action.

As in *The House by the Stable,* Man is shown again as well-inten-tioned but weak, easily influenced, and gullible. He cannot see that Pride has retained her same character though disguised as Self-Respect. Though he killed Immanuel, we are told that he did so "in a sudden brawl" (220), encouraged by Judas, and Man cherishes the memory of Immanuel and honors him. This is why Faith is now in his household, always attended by Grace.

Faith is no vague, other-worldly spirit. She is to be dressed, the author says, "as brightly and sophisticatedly as is possible" (221), in sharp contrast to the veiled, shrouded look of Pride in her disguise. Where Pride flatters with soothing words, Faith speaks crisply and gets to the crux of a situation immediately. She says that Pride is now "prettily disposed to public prayer," by which she means "that sedate / praying to oneself, with oneself too as listener" (228). She tells Man that she can never be friends with Pride and that Man must choose between them. Man foolishly wants to have them both in his house, and only when Faith gets out of the bag and fights with Pride does he begin to see the eternal conflict—and more, the strength of Faith.

Inspired by her, Man is able to throw Hell and put his foot on him. Faith is not only strong but also compassionate. She tells Man kindly that only when the heart breaks, as his seems to when Pride leaves, does one become adult.

Grace is, with Williams's refreshing originality, shown as a young boy. Both he and Faith are said to be older than Hell, though all of them are immortal. Like Faith, Grace is perceptive—he sees, where Gabriel does not, that Pride can never be downed by argument; she must be caught in one of her cheating acts. Grace is never very far from Man. When he is skeptical about Pride's professions of virtue or Man's gullibility, Grace whistles a warning. And when Man is about to succumb to the old allure of Pride, he hears the song Grace is playing and the climax follows swiftly.

The scene with the bag is pure fun—with Gabriel crying out that it is moving, and Grace striking an attitude and saying "sepulchrally," "And where is Faith?" (237). The bag wriggles about, Pride and Hell try to make everyone ignore it, and then the knife blade appears, followed soon by Faith's head. But after the conflict there is a moment of horror, when Pride begs not to be sent away with Hell, to a place "beyond the baboons and the crocodiles, beyond all / but the quicksands that never quite swallow us" (241). A passage like this shows the seriousness of the conflict, which only minutes before had seemed like farce. The play moves constantly between the extremes of seriousness and fun, repugnance and joy.

The "second step" mentioned in the title is what Faith calls "the perseverance into the province of death" (243). Man, in finally sending Pride away, suffers a kind of death. The second step is a death to self, willingly undertaken. In *The House by the Stable* Man's intuitive response to a power of love outside himself is what banishes Pride and Hell, and the Christ is born in Man's house (his heart). But after that, Williams is saying, there comes a time of conscious, painful choice. There must be the will to give up pride, even when it seems only harmless self-respect, because any degree of pride is incompatible with living by faith. Perhaps the most significant lines in *Grab and Grace* are spoken by Man when Grace has told him to decide what to do with Pride and Hell. Man says, "What have I to do with giving sentence? / It seems to me that when I say *I* / or when I think myself someone I am always wrong" (240). He is at last learning to rely on the invisible forces that are always near at hand.

The Three Temptations (1942)

Even more clearly than in *Grab and Grace*, William shows in *The Three Temptations* that man must make a conscious choice of God. A new life is necessary; or, to use one of Williams's favorite expressions, not just the old man on the new way, but a new man.

The Three Temptations is a play for radio, and the new medium made it easier than before for the author to telescope time. Here he shows the temptation of Christ in the wilderness occurring almost simultaneously with the same sorts of temptation *not* being resisted by the three rulers who condemned him—Herod, Pilate, and Caiaphas.

The play begins with three people in the present day talking about what happened in Jerusalem at the time of Christ's ministry. Their voices fade into the crowds surrounding John the Baptist, and we hear the three rulers deciding to send messengers to question John. Immediately after the questioning, the crowds are aware of Jesus, who asks John to baptize him. Then, with only a brief pause, Jesus is with the Evil one, who offers three temptations: the comfort of "flesh"—the desire to turn stones into bread and satisfy hunger; the comfort of glory, or the desire for great reputation and the certainty of success; and the comfort of religion, the urge to test the ever-protecting power of God. All of these Christ rejects. The scene fades into voices crying "Hosanna!" to suggest the triumphal entry into Jerusalem, and there follows another meeting of Pilate, Caiaphas, and Herod, when they make their bargain with Judas. As they talk, the noise of a crowd increases—Jesus has been caught. Pilate's wife Claudia enters and urges him not to touch Jesus, telling of a strange dream she had. Pilate ignores the warning and goes out to give sentence. There is a great silence and darkness, and presently

Judas runs in crying and tries to give back the silver. Claudia also returns, this time to announce that she can no longer live the life of compromise: her dream of Christ has given her courage to choose the Kingdom instead of self.

The Three Temptations emphasizes not only the pain of choice, but man's willful, stubborn refusal to give up anything that makes him comfortable or assured. The three particular ways in which people hold on to comfort, i.e., prefer themselves to Christ, are embodied in the three rulers. They fear any change and have no faith or expectation of anything good or great which might be sought. For them "any crisis is . . . a mistake" (380). Herod is afraid of any threat to his wealth, Pilate fears for his reputation, and Caiaphas takes refuge in his comfortable religion that makes no strenuous demands on him. And these three—money, fame, religion—are the temptations offered to Christ by the Evil one. All of these he rejects in favor of a self-denying, difficult path along which he has no personal gain but allows God to work *through* him. In sharp contrast to his humility and willingness to suffer are the three rulers and Judas, who is called Everyman. All of them choose comfort—whatever is easy and most pleasing to themselves, requiring no self-sacrifice.

John Heath-Stubbs, the editor of Williams's collected plays, finds it "appalling" to have Judas called Everyman.[25] But Judas is a reflection of most people's timid conformity and silent betrayal of their own best insights. Like many, he hides from himself the hideousness of his action under a seemingly modest wish for reasonable consideration by the authorities. Herod sees him as someone who "prefers the quiet temporary comfort of damnation / to the crucifixion of glory" (393).

It is Herod, throughout the play, who has a clear-sighted view of what is really happening. Cynically, he believes that Jesus' call to give up self-interest is not only unwelcome to most people but something to be resisted.

The only character who chooses the difficult way of Christ is Pilate's wife, Claudia. In the dream she has just before Pilate gives judgement, she sees Jesus coming to her bed, looking like each of her friends in turn, each one in pain and agony. And she feels their pains: "I felt my muscles cramp, my bones burn, / my head rack as if thorns stabbed" (396). Her dream is an image of the way of exchange; in the redeemed City no one can suffer alone, and each is concerned for all the others. But as Claudia realizes, this concern is far from the private sort of comfort that the rulers and Judas desire and take for granted. Christ's is a way of life on another level, both demanding and giving more than she had ever imagined. After the crucifixion, only Claudia realizes fully that a judgement has taken place: that Judas and the three rulers, who wanted their own comfort, now have it—and it is hell.

Before looking at the last play, *Terror of Light,* let us see where this discussion of themes in Williams's drama has brought us. The startling statement, "All luck is good," in *the Death of Good Fortune,* can be understood by studying the other plays, which dramatize the qualities men should develop to achieve this understanding.

Archbishop Cranmer learns humility; the Skeleton succeeds in showing him that in and of himself he can do no good thing. In *The House of the Octopus* Anthony, through the approach of martyrdom, finds that his pride in his leadership of the young Church has kept him from a real understanding of God's nature. In *Judgement at Chelmsford* the Church, humbled by seeing its stained and murky past, finds salvation only through giving up all pretensions to worth. Through these plays we see that man becomes significant only as a part of the great pattern of God's glory. Only from within this pattern can he see that all luck is good.

Seed of Adam shows us one character, the Virgin Mary, who has achieved freedom from self-insistence and therefore has a constant awareness of love and glory. In *The House by the Stable* and *Grab and Grace* we are shown specifically how to follow her example. We must give up pride, accept as true the presence of God in our lives, and live by faith and grace.

In *The Three Temptations* the path becomes more fearsome. Williams in this play says that we must give up comfort as well as pride. A wish for comfort means a temptation to think of results first instead of aims, and it must be rejected as Christ rejected it. To have comfort can mean a selfish withdrawal from active exchange.

Terror of Light (1940)

This last play to be considered is the only one of Williams's plays written in prose, and it must be looked on as a first draft, since he intended to rewrite it in verse. It is a play about Pentecost, an account of what might have happened on the day when the Holy Spirit came to the Apostles like a mighty rushing wind and tongues of flame.

The scene is in the orchard of John's house ten days after the crucifixion; all the Apostles are gathered there, with Mary the mother of Jesus and Mary Magdalen. They speak of the election just held to put Matthias in the place of Judas. Saul of Tarsus arrives and is shocked to find Mary Magdalen, the harlot, there. Simon the Magus, another visitor, hopes to obtain knowledge of the "magic" used by Jesus to ascend into heaven. With Simon is Luna, his "instrument of compulsion" (343); her psychic powers, joined with his, can enable him to understand secret and invisible things.

As the Apostles assemble on the roof, only Simon and Luna are left on the stage. To find out what is happening, he puts her into a trance, from which she tells him what she sees: the Apostles, joined by millions of other "companions of the Spirit" (344), are standing like pillars, with light breaking all around them and flames playing in the wind. Then she finds herself sinking to the ocean floor, moving among dead bodies and stones. She is terrified but cannot rise up; instead someone else rises—Judas Iscariot. He says Simon has called him up from Hell, and he speaks bitterly of having his place on earth taken by Matthias. Simon tries, with the authority of his magic staff, to send Judas back to Hell but he cannot. Peter, however, returns and commands him. Judas goes, and as he leaves, Mary Magdalen asks his forgiveness for having been angry with him. Simon then tries to "exchange magic" (353) with Peter. Not succeeding, he prepares to leave, but finds that Luna cannot move; her soul is still down "at the bottom of the light" (355) and neither it nor her body is free. Simon's charms are unavailing to release her. Nor will Peter try to. But Mary Magdalen, full of pity, appeals to the Holy Spirit, offering to live or die in Luna's place, and immediately Luna is free.

Saul, having seen the effect of the flames and wind and voices on the people, rushes in demanding to know what has happened. He prays to God to save them all from blasphemy and evil imagining. Then he abuses Mary Magdalen, disputes with Thomas, and leaves in a fury. Alone, Mary Magdalen and John speak of their love for each other. The last scene is with Mary the Virgin, who tells them she has seen Judas in the garden, and he has repented and agreed to accept Matthias as his substitute. She feels that her work on earth is done now. Having spoken encouragingly to them all, she prepares to die, and her last words, before she faints in John's arms, are, "Blessed be God" (374).

Terror of Light is a very interesting play, containing several ideas that run through most of Williams's work. The most noticeable of these is that of exchange, which is related to the "nothingness" that is a theme in all the plays. Living in Christ, we look to others for our help, and in turn we are divinely enabled to help those who look to us.

So the girl Luna cannot raise herself from the ocean floor, the very hell which is "at the bottom of the terror beyond light" (346). Simon, who ought to help her, finds his magic of no effect here. But Mary Magdalen offers herself. Throwing over Luna the precious veil that Jesus' mother made for her, she says, "Luna, if our Lord wishes you to lie still, then lie on, but if not, then live.—And I will die for you or live for you in the Lord" (357). Luna rises up, and answers their questioning by saying, "There was a woman lying by me, and then both of us lived, both of us" (357). She begs Mary to give her the veil and Mary does so only reluctantly. Despite the miracle of self-sacrifice she has just shown, she still keeps a remnant of the old "somethingness" of pride in her own appearance.

Mary Magdalen has fallen in love romantically with John, and he with her. In spite of a lingering wish to be loved for themselves alone, each of them feels that this new love has come about because they have seen the light of Christ in each other. Mary says to John, "He has exchanged us with each other. I have begun to live in him through you ever since that morning in the garden" (365). John speaks in a similar way to her, saying, "You were the first thing I saw after I had come out of the grave. Everything began to grow again, and everything was new" (366). They are beginning to live, for the first time, in something larger than themselves—in the love that is the substance of all things.

Seen in this way, the relation of John and Mary Magdalen is not embarrassing as it is to Saul in the play and might be to a modern audience.[26] These lovers are not deluded; they are not mistaking a physical attraction for a spiritual experience, as Saul suggests. Instead, they are seeing human love as a type of the divine love that permeates the universe.

Saul, who is shown to be utterly sincere, devoted to God and the Law, knows nothing yet about exchange, but Mary the Virgin suspects that Christ is "implacably determined" (335) to have him, and Thomas also feels that Saul's very passion may bring him to become one of them. He sees that Saul's belligerent faith and his own cool skepticism complement and need each other. When Saul, infuriated by Thomas's mockery, threatens to kill him, Thomas forces him out of the garden but at the same time prophesies that when Saul is one of the Apostles, "we will praise each other in the exchanges of heaven, . . . Scepticism is the need of faith, and faith of scepticism" (364).

The other exchange in the play is that of Matthias, who is only mentioned, for Judas. Judas at first, when he rises from Hell, tries to justify himself. He argues that his temptation had been greater than Peter's and insists that his rights as an Apostle cannot be annulled by death. But this self-assertion does not help him. He remains in agony, and only when his troubled spirit, still walking about John's garden, meets Mary the Virgin does he find salvation. The mercy of God, through Mary, brings Judas to accept the appointment of Matthias. Now she believes he will come to be "glad of substitution and love it" (369), and as he loves it he will be *in* the substitution and therefore healed. "His exclusion shall become his inclusion" (370). The implication here is that Judas, too, will eventually be a part of the web of glory. The slightest movement of the will toward giving up self and repenting of wrongdoing allows the incredible love and mercy to pour forth and bless.

The moving energy of the play is the light named in the title. Like the Flame in *The House of the Octopus,* it represents the Holy

Spirit—but unlike the Flame, the light is not a character in the play; rather, it is an invisible force felt by the characters. Its tremendous power has been felt in Christ, before the play opens—for the lives of all the Apostles and Mary Magdalen were transformed by Him. In spite of radical changes in themselves, however, they still had a fear of death and grieved when Jesus was crucified. Now, when the Spirit comes as a great wind and light, they begin to feel the power that Jesus had as part of themselves. Peter says that "in that light I saw us dead there and living there" (349–50)—the old distinction between life and death has been erased. Now there is nothing but the light or its absence; and the absence, which Peter thinks of as death, is even then not wholly a darkness. Judas says that even among the stones "at the bottom of the universe" (346) there was a "voice moving everywhere in the light" (351).

The power of the light is terrifying. Luna is afraid of it and begs to be taken from the depths where it is. Simon has no power over the light; when he tries to exert his authority over Judas by pronouncing the august names written on his staff, Judas breathes on the staff, saying, "When the light began to move it put an end to this" (349). Peter explains that the tongues of fire were flickering at the light's edges only, for "we could not have borne the light itself" (349), which is the power of creation.

The light is also another name for the glory. Just before Mary's death she tells John that the Spirit has until that day "secluded himself . . . in this flesh, but now he has given himself in a thousand places, and there is, I think, no need of me here. The glory has issued out of Themselves" (370), by whom she means the Apostles, who are to take it wherever they are commanded. They are now indeed aware of what it is to be "nothing"—not important for their own conclusions or actions, not "righteous" in the usual sense of that word, but purveyors of the light or of glory.

This glory has been mentioned in plays already discussed. In *The House of the Octopus* a power beyond the personal self is seen as the "web of glory," a web of relationships based on exchange. The web is a bright diagram, infinitely detailed and exact. In *Judgement at Chelmsford* the image of the web becomes one of the City which is seen by St. Osyth in her vision. Both terms, the web of glory and the City, indicate a way of living in which people "coinhere" or abide in one another in the power of Christ—that is, they practice exchange, for they are in a state of continuous goodwill comparable to being always in love. They are, like Mary in *Seed of Adam* and John and Mary Magdalen in *Terror of Light,* living both in the ordinary world and in another dimension, that of glory.

Chapter Three
The Novels

A dominant theme in Charles Williams's plays is man's relationship to God. As Williams sees him, man, usually unaware of his dependence on God's sustaining love and all-inclusive goodness, feels separate and subject to evil, both within himself and in his world. But God transcends our human ideas of evil, and to understand the nature of His love requires an imaginative leap of faith or a vision of transcendence. It is this vision that the novels communicate. A theme in all of them is the "otherness" that exists in our lives, another dimension that can be discovered in the daily routine. Only a writer intensely aware of both worlds could enable us, as Williams does, to glimpse the power and beauty, danger and glory that exist within our usual experience.

The novels can best be considered in chronological order, for they fall naturally into three groups that coincide with their time sequence. The first novel he wrote is the least effective, the next four have a common theme, and the last two, though retaining some of the earlier themes, are more related to each other than to the previous novels.

Shadows of Ecstasy (1933)

Shadows of Ecstasy was written first but only published after Williams had become fairly well known. Its plot seems relevant to today's world, though it is also rather incredible.

Roger Ingram and his wife Isabel, with their friend Sir Bernard Travers, become acquainted at a lecture with Nigel Considine, who later reveals that he has lived for two hundred years. He, it turns out, is responsible for revolts in Africa and the killing of white missionaries there. Now his Africans are invading London. All dark-skinned people become suspect, and Roger and Isabel rescue a Zulu king, Inkamasi, from a hostile crowd. By so doing they are brought into further contact with Considine, who has hypnotic power over the king and holds him captive. A friend of Sir Bernard, the priest Caithness, persuades Sir Bernard to help him remove Inkamasi, who is a Christian, from Considine's house. The next day Caithness takes Inkamasi to a mass at Lambeth, where the spell upon him is broken.

Meanwhile, Africans are bombing London and fighting in the streets. Philip, Sir Bernard's son, is caught in a race riot at the home of Simon Rosenberg, whose recent mysterious death seems also connected with Considine. Despite appearances against Considine, Roger Ingram feels he must accompany him when he leaves London for his retreat in a house by the sea. Considine compels Inkamasi also to go with him, and Caithness goes along to protect the Zulu. At the retreat, Considine persuades Inkamasi to accept a "royal death," but when the king dies, Considine is also killed by one of his followers, Mottreux, with the approval of Caithness. The African liberation movement collapses, and Roger returns, saddened, to London.

Ecstasy, in the novel, is the power that one feels when in love, a sense of surpassing energy, a heightened awareness of everything. The "shadows" of the title are what Williams sometimes calls images, the external symbols of the power—not the thing itself. Such symbols are man's creative works and his relationships with other people—all made possible by the emotional and imaginative energy within him.

It is this energy, or ecstasy, that the chief character, Nigel Considine, has used to prolong his life for two hundred years. There is a strangeness about Considine. People notice a quiet intensity in him, a physical stillness. He seldom moves. He has preserved his life by not wasting any psychic energy, turning it inwards instead, filling himself with the consciousness of it so that his body does not deteriorate. He and his followers believe that they have the secret of immortality.

Considine's purpose is to be superior to the greater part of mankind. Like most of Williams's villains, he wants power over other people, and he thinks that the person who masters death will be lord of the world. When the novel opens, Considine has gained control of the Africans, and he wants to free Africa from all European influence. As a step in this direction, he has sanctioned the killing of white missionaries, giving them the "perfect gift" (42) of martyrdom. He now proposes to terrify the English into submission by invading London with his African warriors.

Considine's methods as a conqueror are so subtle that he even seems to deceive himself as to his true purpose. His rationalization of the killing of the missionaries is similar to his explanation of the murder of Inkamasi. Inkamasi, in the African war, has been dispossessed of his realm; he can no longer return to Africa as a king. To live in England is now equally distasteful to him; after the uprising in London he will be suspect and may be imprisoned along with other black people. He has always believed he should never give up his kingship and Considine, who seems to share his romantic feeling for the whole mystique of kingship, offers him a "royal death." But *does* Considine share this feeling? Or is he only finding a sure way of disposing of an enemy? Is his whole exaltation of emotion and ecstasy, his training of "initiates," and his apppeal to poetic feelings, merely a splendid façade for his ruthless drive to dominate? If it is a façade, he has succeeded in disguising his own motives to himself, and perhaps Williams is saying that all conquerors do so.

On the other hand, there is the fact that he has overcome death. Nevertheless he cannot ward off a sudden attack, and it is a surprise shot that does kill him in the end, although he has kept his body from deteriorating through age in the usual way. As a forceful idea Considine is effective.[1] His belief in the "ecstasy of vivid experience" (40) and his exemplification of that belief have convinced the group of white followers, whom he calls the "adepts," and the masses of black people who almost worship him.

Also in his favor is the fact that Roger Ingram, a sensitive and intelligent man, is willing to follow him. Some of the book's most vivid passages are composed of Roger's reflections as he accompanies Considine to his retreat by the sea and tries to follow his instructions about turning all emotion back into himself.

Yet Considine has a quality that his disciple, Mottreux, calls inhuman, and it is this deliberate self-sufficiency, this cold disregard of human values, that makes him scarcely believable as a person. Standing in his car as it rolls through the tumultuous streets where the blacks are killing themselves and one another to frantic cries of "Death for the Deathless One," Considine says calmly to his companions, "As for my Africans they ask for death and they shall have death . . . I do not pity them; they are not the adepts . . ." (152).

With similar coldness he arranges for the murder of Inkamasi because royalty, along with love and poetry, is one of the "channels whereby the passion and imagination of man's heart become revealed to him" (207); and his adepts, to strengthen themselves, must feed on the spectacle of Inkamasi's death.

It is Inkamasi who gives the clue to Considine's ultimate failure. Although he has apparently been dominated by Considine for many years, in his inmost self the Zulu king has never submitted to this domination. He has rejected Considine's insistence on emotion and imagination as the sole saviors of mankind because, he says, "I do not think mankind can be saved without intellect and without God" (112). In *Shadows of Ecstasy* the power of religion and the power of intellect are shown to be as important as that of imagination.

Intellect is represented by Sir Bernard, who refuses to accompany Considine and his party to the house by the sea, saying, "We've come out of the jungle and I for one am not going back" (148). Sir Bernard represents Williams's belief in the value of skepticism. His calm irony makes for freedom of thought in his household, where people are encouraged to believe whatever is true for them.

Williams's treatment of the power of religion is interesting in that he pictures Caithness, the priest, as far from admirable. He is highly emotional, almost fanatical, and he loses sight of one of the basic principles of Christianity when he becomes a tacit accomplice in the killing of Considine. Unlike Sir Bernard, he can at times forget reason and conscience; they are swallowed up in zeal.

Yet the power of God, as shown in the novel, is not dependent on the strength of its advocates. Inkamasi sitting in Considine's house in a hypnotic trance, is not roused by Caithness's commands that he wake; but he is affected by the words invoking the Trinity and calling, "Inkamasi, Inkamasi, by the faith you hold, by the baptism and the Body of Christ, I bid you wake" (93). In the moments following, Sir Bernard and Caithness are able to half lead, half push the sleeping Zulu out of the house and to the waiting car. His full release comes next day, when the Archbisop conducts a mass at a chapel in Lambeth Palace.

The value of the mass is seen not only in the restoration of Inkamasi's right mind and action, but in its effect on the mind and feelings of Philip, Sir Bernard's son. Philip, though not a believer, kneels on a chair during the service and becomes aware of a power he has not previously known. He cannot understand all that is said, but he experiences an emotion he has sometimes known while waiting for his fiancée Rosamond—"entire expectation yet mingled with complete repose and certainty" (101). His belief that his love for Rosamond belongs to an eternal order of things finds an echo in the service. He remembers how once, in the house at Hampstead, he had seen Rosamond's arm outstretched along a chair back, and it seemed to hold an immense significance. Here in the mass is the same significance, an awareness of something stable, permanent.

The reader now begins to understand religion and love, or God *as* love, to be a more certain and comprehensive power than Considine's ecstasy or Sir Bernard's reason. By ignoring religion Considine fails, not only in ruling the will of Inkamasi, but in his whole attempt to dominate the world.

Shadows of Ecstasy can be seen, then, as a study in various kinds of power, a theme that recurs in the later novels. Its ideas are not its strength; Williams was to treat them more effectively elsewhere. Nor is the characterization very remarkable. It is its exuberant pace that is the novel's chief merit. Especially memorable scenes, Dickensian in their vivid detail, are those of the crowd attacking the Rosenberg house, and the panic in the streets of London after the blacks' raid. In a scene where Considine escapes from the police who have come to arrest him there is a suggestion of supernatural power existing alongside or within the everyday scene—something that Williams was to develop more fully in other novels.

War in Heaven (1930)

In 1930 Williams was writing many reviews of thrillers, so it is not surprising that his second novel begins like a detective story, with a dead body lying in a publishing house. The murderer, not discovered immediately, is Gregory Persimmons, who studies black magic and has a lust for supernatural power. Through Sir Giles Tumulty, Persimmons learns that the original Holy Grail (spelled Graal) is now at the parish church at Fardles. He asks Tumulty to remove from his book on *Sacred Vessels in Folklore* a paragraph indicating the Graal's whereabouts. Before the paragraph can be deleted in proof, however, it is shown to the Archdeacon of Fardles by Kenneth Mornington, a clerk in the publishing house.

There ensues a contest for the Graal between Persimmons and the Archdeacon. Persimmons steals it and uses it to get in touch with the soul of a child, Adrian, son of Lionel and Barbara Rackstraw. He hopes to offer Adrian's soul to Satan. The Graal is recovered by the Archdeacon with the help of Mornington and the young Duke of the North Ridings, who drive with it to London, hotly pursued by Persimmons and the police. Two of Persimmons's allies, a Greek at a disreputable chemist's shop and Manasseh, a Jew, send forth evil vibrations to destroy the Graal, but the Archdeacon, Mornington, and the Duke spend a night praying for it, and it remains intact.

Now Prester John, the Oriental priest-king of the Middle Ages, returns to earth to protect the Graal; he appears as a mysterious young man in gray. He saves the life of Barbara Rackstraw, whom Persimmons has deliberately poisoned with a magical ointment. Through Prester John, too, Inspector Colquhoun discovers that the murdered man was Pattison, whom Persimmons had employed to commit petty crimes.

The Graal, through a ruse, has been obtained by Manasseh and the Greek. Mornington and the Duke go to the chemist's shop to retrieve it but Mornington is swiftly murdered there by magic, and the Duke is forced to write to the Archdeacon, summoning him to the shop. When the Archdeacon comes, he is bound down to the floor and the Graal placed on his chest, in preparation for a ceremony of black magic, in which his soul will be joined to that of the murdered Pattison; thus the Archdeacon will lose his identity and integrity. But the nefarious rite is interrupted by Prester John, who releases the captives and warns Persimmons that he must die in the place of Pattison. Persimmons gives himself up to the police. The next day, at a mass at Fardles church, the Archdeacon dies on the steps of the altar, and Prester John and the chalice vanish.

As can readily be seen, Williams has in this novel combined the suspense of the murder mystery with an interest in religion and the occult. What is not apparent from the plot summary is the mystical insight that marks the novel.

In all his novels Williams is concerned with the struggle between good and evil. He takes the title of this one from a verse in Revelation: "And there was war in heaven: Michael and his angels fought against the dragon; and the dragon fought and his angels, and prevailed not."[2] The struggle is seen as going on constantly, with the war on earth a replica of that in heaven, a series of battles or skirmishes in which evil is always overcome but has always to be opposed again.

Central to the war, and the object for which both sides contend, is the Holy Graal. Williams makes it seem quite plausible that this legendary chalice, from which Jesus and His disciples drank at the Last Supper, should now be found in a little country church in England. Until examined closely it looks much like any other chalice; but to the Duke and Kenneth Mornington it has vast significance, suggesting religious wars and the romances of King Arthur and his knights. Both forces in the contest seek the Graal because it is a storehouse of spiritual power. As such it can be used for either good or evil purposes. Gregory Persimmons works by means of magic, reversing and distorting the real power of God. His allies, Manasseh and the Greek, work in the same way but for a different end. Their purpose is not to make use of the Graal, but to destroy it.

For the Archdeacon, the Graal signifies at times the very presence of God, the supernatural breaking through into the natural. When he looks at the chalice standing on a bracket in Gregory's house he hears an unearthly music, "not from without, or indeed from within, from some non-spatial, non-temporal, non-personal existence" (117).

Although Gregory Persimmons is evil, seeking to use the Graal for his own ends—which are chiefly the harassment of the good—he is an essentially religious man. He is mistaken but truly religious in that he believes in prayer and sacrifice to his god. His purpose is to destroy instead of to create, to manipulate people instead of respecting them. But he is religious in that he believes in a power beyond himself that makes a response to him. When he anoints his body with a magical ointment and goes into a trance, he attends a witches' sabbath, where his spirit joins other spirits like himself, those eager to prey upon and destroy the innocent.

Gregory dies in recompense for the man he murdered, but his soul is saved. This is because, unlike his allies in evil, he is not hardened in the ways of negation. He has sought for spiritual power in order to amuse himself, and to hurt and destroy. But then he meets the Greek, highly experienced in magic and utterly disillusioned with everything; and he meets Manasseh, who can never destroy enough, never be satisfied and is therefore always frustrated. Gregory begins to doubt his own purpose and methods. These two have gone farther along the road he is travelling; what have they gained? He has also met the Archdeacon and understood something of his unshakable inner peace. Gregory is baffled by this peace, as it seems far beyond any pleasure he can ever experience himself. Also, he is shocked and a bit frightened by the means used to destroy Kenneth Mornington. "He shrank from the face of the sorcerer . . . A sickness crept within him; was this the end of victory and lordship and the Sabbath, and this the consummation of the promises and of desire?" (217).

Of the other evil characters, Sir Giles Tumulty, though taking a less active part, is the spark that ignites much of Gregory's abominable work. His name suggests tumult or chaos, and it is his delight to stir up disorder: "He had himself an utter disbelief in God and devil, but he found these anthropomorphic conceptions interesting, and to push or delay any devotee upon the path was entertainment to a mind too swiftly bored" (82). He looks at people as if they were all specimens in a laboratory, with no concern for their feelings.

And yet, he is not, in this novel, a lost soul (his self-destruction is to come later, in *Many Dimensions*) because he is sincerely interested in things outside himself; he has the true scholar's curiosity that overrides self-concern.

As the evil forces are manipulated by Gregory Persimmons, so the Archdeacon stands as the chief champion of good. It is characteristic of Williams's irony that he gives this role to an ordinary and slightly comical character. The Archdeacon is a small, stout, and rather dainty man. He wears gaiters and gold-rimmed glasses and walks sedately; his manner is placid and serene. As the story progresses, the reader realizes in him a keen intelligence and, more important, a will that is always under the direction of God. He is constantly living on two levels: active and perceptive in worldly affairs, he is at the same time always in touch with the world of spirit. He often recites or sings softly under his breath a psalm of thanksgiving, a habit that others find rather disconcerting.

Like all the saints, the Archdeacon is in the habit of frequently withdrawing his attention from the world, to be in touch with God in the silence. In this silence he receives direction and knows what action he must take. He knows when to remove the Graal from Gregory's house, and he knows when the evil thoughts of Manasseh and the Greek are trying to make the Graal disintegrate. On this occasion his guidance comes swiftly. Suddenly aware of danger to the Graal, he calls to Mornington and the Duke: "Pray that He who made the universe may sustain the universe, that in all things there may be delight in the justice of His will" (140). Their prayer is successful because it is begun so promptly, and we realize that the Archdeacon has trained himself to be always ready, at God's disposal, listening and watching to know how he can be used. Again he receives guidance when Gregory comes to summon him to London. He does not give an immediate answer, though he suspects an evil intent behind the request. Instead of saying he will or will not go, he says he does not know yet, and when Gregory has gone he "went back to his study, shut the door, and gave himself up to interior silence and direction" (236).

His decision to go to London marks the climax of the war. There, in the chemist's shop where Kenneth Mornington was murdered a short time before, the last battle takes place. And the ordeal for the Archdeacon is like a crucifixion. He knows it is God's will that he is there, but he no longer feels supported by God's power. He feels abandoned, as Christ did on the cross: ". . . now, as he faced his enemies, he felt the interior loss which had attacked him at other stages of his pilgrimage grow into a final overwhelming desolation" (240). The similarity to the cross is strengthened in that he is bound and stretched out on the floor, and the chalice full of blood is, for the purpose of the magic spell, placed on his chest. He feels his body weakening. The room is very dark: "the darkness increased and moved and swirled around them" (240). Something like this, Williams seems to say, must have been Christ's state on the cross in the darkness.

We see the Archdeacon in his moments of joy, of stress, and of agony. By the end of the novel, the figure who appeared a bit ridiculous at first has become a hero.

His allies, Kenneth Mornington and the Duke of the North Ridings, are more briefly sketched, as are all the other lesser characters. As in *Shadows of Ecstasy,* Williams portrays them with a few swift strokes. Both Mornington and the Duke are romantics, idealistic and warmhearted, with the impetuosity of youth. Mornington, enraged at one of Sir Giles's irreverent remarks, gets into a fist fight with him and not only loses his job but is thrown out of the publishing house. The Duke, on hearing that Sir Giles had "insulted God," is equally indignant. They are only calmed when the Archdeacon says that one can no more insult God than he can "pull His nose" (135). Their enthusiasm in the defense of good takes the young men to the chemist's shop, where Mornington meets what can be seen as a martyr's death.

Among the minor characters, Mr. Batesby, the talkative clergyman who assists the Archdeacon, reminds us of Jane Austen's equally boring but comic Miss Bates in *Emma.* Mr. Batesby's conversation is sprinkled with garbled quotations from poetry and the Bible. His are the last words in the novel, which give an ironic twist to the impressive scene of the Archdeacon's death that we have just witnessed. He laments that the Archdeacon has been "cut down like a palm-tree and thrust into the oven" (256).

The mysterious figure called Prester John is a legendary person, not known certainly to have existed, but famous in Europe in the Middle Ages as "a Christian conqueror and potentate of enormous power and splendour, who combined the characters of priest and king, and ruled over vast dominions in the far East."[3] Williams takes this phantom figure and makes him appropriately inconspicuous in a modern setting as an ordinary-looking young man in gray. He seems at times to materialize out of the evening sky or to fade into the garden wall or flower bed. An "otherness" about him makes him rather like an angel visitor.

He arouses different reactions in people; those who are endeavoring to be good welcome him; those intent on evil react to him with hostility. Gregory takes an immediate dislike to him. Sir Giles is more curious about him than hostile, though he feels uncomfortable in his presence. Barbara, Kenneth, and the Duke are full of joy when he appears and feel they have seen him before, though they cannot recall just where. He warns the Archdeacon of his coming ordeal, telling him to be courageous. Prester John can be thought of as a God-bearer, an outward manifestation of an inner grace. He is a real person but at the same time he is more than himself.

His action in the story is crucial. He appears in Fardles just after the all-night vigil of the Archdeacon and his friends at the Duke's house in London. He has come to protect the Graal and to help all those others who also revere it. To that end he restores Barbara Rackstraw to health, thus bringing one of Persimmons's evil purposes to nothing. He brings the Inspector and Mr. Batesby together in a seemingly casual conversation that reveals to the Inspector the identity of Pattison, the murdered man, which in turn discloses Persimmons's intent to murder him. Prester John says to Kenneth Mornington, "To-night thou shalt be with Me in Paradise" (203),[4] thus helping the reader to see, beyond the shock of Mornington's death, the eternal purpose of God being worked out. Most important, when evil seems at the height of its power, Prester John rescues both the Archdeacon and Graal.

If the novel is read only for the surface story, Prester John may seem a flaw in the construction—too much a "god from the machine," someone brought in at the last moment to save the good people and punish the bad so that there will be a happy ending. But such a reading would ignore Williams's basic belief that, despite appearances to the contrary, the God who is love is in complete charge of the universe. The irresistible power of good is always at work, and Prester John, who comes and goes like the sunshine, is only an indication of that invisible power.

It is the splendor and glory of God, seen near the end of the novel, that reveal evil, for all its apparent strength, as powerless. There have been glimpses earlier of supernatural grace, as in Prester John's words to Barbara after her illness, "Believe certainly that this universe carries its salvation in its heart" (203). But the full majesty and joyousness of the invisible world of good is best shown in two apocalyptic scenes near the end. Williams makes these scenes tremendously exciting.

The first scene comes when Prester John appears in the chemist's shop to rescue the Archdeacon. Just when the Archdeacon's soul seems on the point of being lost, distorted, or destroyed by the magic spell, the Graal on his chest is transformed, and the revelation of God comes as light, energy, and music: "blast upon blast of trumpets shook the air; the Graal blazed with fiery tumult before them; and its essence . . . awoke in its own triumphant and blinding power" (244). The Archdeacon becomes aware, as his bonds fall away, of an "infinite chorus," and one voice above all, chanting in an unknown tongue which, though foreign, also seems to him the familiar words of the psalm. " 'Let them give thanks whom the Lord hath redeemed,' a great voice sang, and from all about it, striking into light and sound at once the answer came: 'for His mercy endureth for ever' " (245).

The second scene is at the very end, when Prester John, with the Archdeacon in attendance, celebrates mass in the church at Fardles. The church bell ringing for the service sounds "higher and more remote and more clear than any bell they had heard before" (252). Only a few people are in the congregation, but Barbara and the Duke feel invisible presences and can almost see "a helmed and armoured shape, outlandish robes, and the glint of many crowns" (252–53), though these people seem always to be just to one side or in a remote corner. Barbara hears her son Adrian's voice and that of Prester John but also other voices singing and chanting the responses.

At the elevation of the Host, there is a profound stillness: "All sound ceased; all things entered into an intense suspension of being; nothing was anywhere at all but He" (254). Then, when the priest-king moves his hands, light and color from the Graal flood the church, and the whole universe, earth and stars and planets seem to be moving "in light and darkness and peace" (255). The priest-king calls three times, the Archdeacon leaves his stall and begins to mount the steps. But immediately he sinks down in death, and all the supernatural presences vanish: "The sunlight shone upon an altar as bare as the pavement before it; without violence, without parting, the Graal and its Lord were gone" (255).

Barbara and the others feel the rightness of the Archdeacon's death. "I suppose they will say he had a weak heart," the Duke murmurs (256), but he and Lionel know that their friend has gone on to a greater glory. His work on earth is done. Williams is perhaps suggesting, in his death, a continued parallel to the story of Christ. If the Archdeacon's ordeal in the chemist's shop may be compared to Christ's crucifixion, his rescue by Prester John signifies the resurrection: he is saved from his enemies and taken up into heaven with the Graal.

In this last scene in the church Williams's power of narration, which was evident in his earlier novel, is used with greater skill for a different purpose, one that informs all his best work. As the Archdeacon dies, we have a sense of the utter reality of the unseen world, breaking through to transform the ordinary world, filling it with glory.

Many Dimensions (1931)

In the next novel Williams again used an object as a center of power and of conflict between forces of good and evil. The object this time is a sacred Stone from the crown of King Solomon (Williams uses the Mohammedan name for Solomon—Suleiman ben Daood).

Sir Giles Tumulty buys the Stone from a Persian, and despite warnings of its danger, experiments with it, finding that it can move people in both space and time, can help one to read thoughts, and can be multiplied indefinitely without losing its original size. Stones made from the original one are called Types and have its same power.

Those who hope to exploit the Stone are Sir Giles and his nephew, Reginald; Angus Sheldrake, an American millionaire; and the Mayor of Rich, the town where the Stone's healing properties are discovered. The Mayor wishes the Stone to be given to suffering humanity, but he is opposed by those working in transport industries, who say the Stone will make trains, ships, and other normal methods of transport obsolete.

Lord Arglay, the Lord Chief Justice, and his secretary Chloe Burnett sense from the first a religious quality in the Stone and do not want it exploited. When Sir Giles sends Pondon, a laboratory assistant, into the past by means of the Stone, Lord Arglay and Chloe use their Type to rescue him and return him to the present. In revenge on them for this interference, Sir Giles sends a Persian to steal Chloe's Type from her bedroom at night. She hears the intruder but will not use the Stone to save herself. The intruder is mysteriously destroyed. Soon after, Reginald meets a violent death, and Sir Giles is sucked down into the depths of the Stone and dies in agony.

Lord Arglay is called upon to decide what should be done with the Stone and its Types. He decides that the world is not yet ready for the Stone—it must be returned to its rightful place outside our world. Chloe agrees to be a "path" for the Stone's return. As she holds it in her hands, all the other Types enter it through her body and go thence to the invisible world. She seems to faint, all her vital powers withdrawn. For nine months she lies in a coma, tenderly cared for by Lord Arglay. Then she dies. Sadly but resolutely, Lord Arglay returns to his work on a book on organic law.

This is a rather difficult novel, one that might put off the casual reader who is unwilling to think about the complexities of travel in time or the psychological subtleties of one person seeing into and through the mind of another person. But to those who persist in reading it, it offers another glimpse of an expanded universe.

The title suggests Christ's words in the fourteenth chapter of St. John: "In my Father's house are many mansions," with their suggestion that God moves in ways beyond our understanding. The whole tone of the book is one of opening to our sight wider possibilities: life is more mysterious than we have realized, and God is infinitely beyond our conceptions of space and time—He moves in other dimensions.

The sheer wonder of the story, the appeal of magic as in a fairy story, is the first thing to attract a reader. Initially, the Stone is seen in its ability to move a person from place to place. Reginald, eager to prove its powers to Lord Arglay, places the crown, with its inset Stone, on his head, and wishes himself in Lord Arglay's flat at Lancaster Gate. Once there, he picks up some pages of manuscript to prove where he has been, wishes himself back at Sir Giles's flat in Ealing, and within five minutes he is presenting the pages to Lord Arglay. Another such trial by Lord Arglay himself convinces him.

Then there is the equally amazing demonstration of how the Stone can be divided. Reginald tries at first to take a chip off it with a chisel, but finds he need not use force. It divides immediately, making an exact replica of itself. The possibility of endless multiplication of the Stone disturbs Lord Arglay, but Reginald, after the initial shock, sees only the greater profit to be gained from selling more Stones.

The next marvel discovered is the Stone's ability to send people backward or forward in time. Here the danger of its use becomes obvious. For if someone holding or wearing the Stone wishes himself back to a day before, he will presumably live through that day endlessly: as soon as he gets through that day, he will be back at the point where he willed to return to it and will again wish on the Stone and again go back. He will be caught in the past. Sir Giles, whose curiosity exceeds his humanity, is too cautious to make this experiment himself, but without scruple he persuades Pondon, a poor young laboratory assistant, to wish himself back into the past, and Pondon disappears.

Then, careless of what is happening to Pondon, Sir Giles and his associate, Palliser, take two more Types of the Stone and wish themselves forward in time half an hour. When they begin, the clock shows 11:30 A.M. They have a curious feeling of dizziness, and the next thing they know is Palliser taking leave of a police inspector who came to inquire about Pondon. Sir Giles is exasperated, for he remembers what happened in that half hour—"He remembered the knocking, the caretaker, the entrance of the inspector to whom Palliser was talking . . ." (90), and yet if he had really gone forward immediately to 12 o'clock, he would have lost a half hour, and the things he remembered did not happen. He reflects angrily, "How the hell could I remember if it hadn't happened? There'd be nothing to remember. . . . But at twelve I should remember. Then if it's come off—I remember what hasn't happened. I'm in a delusion, I'm mad" (90). The reader labors after Giles and the author, in a now-you-see-it, now-you-don't frame of mind.

Lord Arglay, whose concern for justice is as strong as Tumulty's indifference to suffering, uses the Stone, first, to see into Sir Giles's mind and find out the truth of what he has suspected—that Giles was actually sending someone into the past. Through the power of the Stone he can watch what is happening, but he can do nothing to stop it: "It was looking out, his mind, through Giles Tumulty's eyes; it was Giles Tumulty's desire that it knew . . . [but his own mind] must act in its own medium; on the crowd of diabolic curiosities that surged around it, it could produce no effect" (62). And so he shuts out the mind of Giles and returns to his own consciousness.

But he worries about Pondon and longs to rescue him. This he is able to do with Chloe's help. Both he and Chloe are coming, each in his own way, to a better understanding of God, or of the Stone as God's representative. They begin to see that the Stone is greater than time; it *contains* time. If, as Lord Arglay says to Chloe, all the Types of the Stone are really one, then the Type that Pondon is holding is the same as the one they now hold; they have a point of contact with him that is outside time.

Lord Arglay sits holding the Stone, and Chloe puts her hand over his. Their separate reveries as they sit there are given in detail; and Chloe's trance is full of pain. She feels herself growing old. She feels darkness and cold despair: "All the pain of heart-ache she had ever known, all negligences, desertions, and betrayals, were gathered here, and were shutting themselves up with her alone" (139). Her psychic anguish seems to enable Arglay to make contact with Pondon. For suddenly he has a sensation of feeling Pondon's hand on his; then there is "a faint crash somewhere, a sensation of rushing violence" (142). We understand that Pondon has crashed through into the present time.

An equally spectacular virtue of the Stone is its ability to heal disease. Oliver Doncaster, who finds one of the Types, shows it to old Mrs. Ferguson, the mother of his landlady, who has been in bed for a year, paralyzed from the waist down. As she holds it, Mrs. Ferguson says plaintively that she wishes she could run as well now as she did when a child, and immediately she finds herself able to get out of her bed and walk. She shows the Stone to her sister, who is instantly cured of her asthma, and the news goes quickly around the village of Rich. Williams describes, in a modern setting, a scene comparable to biblical accounts of the sick crowding around Christ.

Thereafter the worldly powers—government, business interests, and scientists—struggle for authority over the Stone. In contrast, Chloe and Lord Arglay believe that it should never be used at all. By now, the reader wonders what this Stone really is, and does the author intend us to take it seriously?

Undoubtedly he does. Like the Graal in *War in Heaven,* the Stone looks both ordinary and mysterious. It is small, "a cubical stone measuring about half an inch every way" (7) and of a milky color flaked with gold; on it, not engraved but seeming to be the actual substance of it, are the four letters of the Tetragrammaton, the ancient Hebrew name for God. We see it first as this curious relic. But it does not look the same at all times. It seems to be strangely alive. After Chloe refuses to save herself by means of the Stone, it becomes more radiant: ". . . its size was no greater but its depth seemed, as in some great jewel, to be infinitely increased . . . It expanded within . . ." (229). Again, just before Sir Giles is destroyed by the Stone, it seems to him to be expanding into "coils of moving and alternated splendour and darkness" (243).

Like the Graal, then, the Stone is both itself and the power of God. We are told of its divine nature when the Hajji Ibrahim, a wise old Persian, says that the Stone is "the First Matter . . . from wich all things are made—spirits and material things" (56). He also calls it indivisible; therefore, it is unity, or the Unity that is God—all sufficient; so it can heal, and containing within it all times and all places, make it possible for someone in touch with it to come and go within it as he wishes. The Stone is everything, and everything is in it. And, of course, because it contains all, it is appropriately called the End of Desire. It is no wonder that the Hajji is enraged to think of Sir Giles threatening to "divide the Indivisible for his own ends" (57), or that Chloe, who is of a religious bent, begins to reverence it.

Thinking of the Stone as an image of God, we can see why it allows itself to be multiplied by men and used by them. Such humility also characterized Jesus of Nazareth, that other representative of God. The Stone gives its power freely, as Jesus did. The Hajji tells Lord Arglay, "it will do anything you ask it—with all your heart. But you must will truly and sincerely" (56).

There is another parallel to Jesus. The Stone, powerful as it is, cannot unite its divided Types into one Stone again. It was said of Jesus at his crucifixion, "He saved others; himself he cannot save."[5] Similarly, the Hajji explains that the Stone "will do nothing for itself of itself, neither divide nor reunite" (58). But he adds that the Stone can be returned to its original Unity in the invisible world if some person agrees to be the vehicle for that return, willing to unite himself with the Stone in God. As the story makes clear, the Stone cannot remain in the world. People are not ready for it; they quarrel over it, seeking to use it for their own selfish purposes. It must be returned, and Chloe becomes the means whereby it can go. The Stone is returned by means of a human will and human body.

Chloe is a natural choice for a path for the Stone. Her gentleness at first hides the strength of her will, but early in the story we are told that she is always seeking, rather wistfully, for something greater than herself. She is attracted by the mystery and beauty of the Stone and at the same time by its vulnerability. When Lord Arglay gives her one of the Types for safekeeping, she cherishes it.

She feels that it represents a transcendent power which is wholly good. To her friend Frank Lindsay, when he taunts her about not lending him the Stone, she says she would never use it for herself, not "to buy myself food if I was starving" (162). The temptation to lend it to Frank, to help him pass his examination, is unpleasant; she thinks that she will lose his friendship, and he tries to make her feel selfish in not giving it up. But she is quite clear about her duty.

A greater temptation to use the Stone comes when Prince Ali gets into her room at night and attempts to steal it. Lying awake in the dark, she hears the door handle turn and believes someone has come for the Stone. Her hands close over it under her pillow, and she remains passive. Holding the Stone, she could easily will herself to be elsewhere, out of reach of the intruder. But that would be to exploit it for her own safety. As she is not in the habit of praying, she can only remember "Thy will be done," and she tries to let the Stone do as it will with her. She says, "Do, or do not," i.e., save me, or do not save me; let it be according to your will. In that moment of her complete surrender she is saved, and the power of the Stone is revealed as light and music: "The light grew suddenly around her . . . a vibration went through her, as if a note of music had been struck along her whole frame, and far off she heard as it were a single trumpet at the gate of Suleiman with a prolonged blast saluting the dawn" (219).

Thus the Stone, or the light within it, protects her in her need. The light apparently is a double thing. It can illumine—it is, the Hajji says, the light of wisdom given to King Solomon that enabled him to see the truth in perplexing situations—and it is wholly beautiful. But it can also blast and destroy. Because Chloe has sincerely sought to serve the Stone, it turns its awful power on any who try "in anger or hatred or evil desire" to hurt her (228). Then its light is destructive. When Prince Ali is found by a police constable he is not inside Chloe's house at all; his body is lying outside on the doorstep, "burnt as if by lightning and broken as if cast from an immense distance" (220).

In the same way, it is a pitiless light that destroys Sir Giles when, sitting in his room, he breaks out into rage and damns both Chloe and the Stone. In one of the most horrifying passages in Williams's writing, we see, through Giles's eyes, the Stone growing larger, "dilating and deepening," and it becomes like a living thing, "riven in all its parts by a subdued but increasing light" (243). It seems to grow until it occupies all the room, and its light becomes pain in all his nerves and sinews. Soon he becomes caught in the Stone's vast coils and is sucked down to his death. His body, when it is found, is, like Ali's, "pierced and burnt all over as if by innumerable needle-points of fire" (246).

Since the light of the Stone, that destroys Giles, is the same glorious light that can enlighten and protect, Williams clearly is *not* saying that Tumulty is punished by a cruel and vengeful god. Rather, because Tumulty has rejected love, which is light, and sought only to use other people for his own purposes, he now sees the light in reverse—in horror and pain.

Such is the double nature of the Stone that is the moving force of the novel and the power to which Chloe gives her life. To understand what happens to her in the end, one must consider her relation to Lord Arglay.

Lord Arglay, who is twice Chloe's age, is different from her and complements her character. Where she is idealistic and eager, he is detached and ironical, though open to truth in whatever form it may appear. He has always believed in reason and law, and at times he has wondered if "the nature of law was also the nature of God" (59). There might well be, he thinks, a power quite outside his reasoning mind. Repelled, as Chloe is, by the spectacle of people squabbling over possession of the Stone, he decides to ally himself with her and believe in the Stone's transcendent nature—or, to believe in God.

Chloe's feeling for Lord Arglay is more than hero-worship; she finds in him sophistication in the true sense of that word; his maturity and stability of character make her young admirers, such as Frank Lindsay, seem shallow and unsatisfactory. Lord Arglay admires Chloe as a skillful secretary and a sensitive human being, and as the story goes on he becomes more attached to her. Their friendship is entirely platonic, and the sneers and innuendoes made by Sir Giles about them only serve to emphasize the purity of their relationship.

As Chloe becomes more devoted to the Stone, seeking to know its meaning, the "End of Desire," and Lord Arglay encourages and supports her, they become types or images of the Virgin Mary and Joseph, her protector. Williams says:

As if a Joseph with more agnostic irony than tradition usually allows him sheltered and sustained a Mary of a more tempestuous past than the Virgin-Mother is believed to have either endured or enjoyed, so Lord Arglay considered, as far as it was clear to him, his friend's progress towards the End of Desire (194).

Together they must make the decision about the Stone's return to God or "the Unity." Chloe is willing to be the means of its return, but Lord Arglay, in his understanding, must move before she can. After much deliberation, he decides that they will offer Chloe as the path for the Stone to "fulfil itself through us if that is its desire" (258). Since Williams has compared them to Mary and Joseph, in the passage above, we are reminded of his other comment on Jesus' parents in *Seed of Adam:* "A heart of purity and a mind of justice to be integrity." In the action that Chloe and Lord Arglay undertake, we can think of Justice making possible the movement of Love; or, the Law, the old understanding of God, making way for the new understanding of God as love.

The action of returning the Stone is described in detail. Lord Arglay hands it to Chloe, and she presents to it, in intercession, all those who, like Frank Lindsay and Giles Tumulty, have tried to exploit it. As she does so, Arglay is aware for a fleeting moment that the outer world, seen through the window, *is* the Stone (for everything is God). Then he sees the various Types merging into the Stone, passing through Chloe and into the Stone in her hands. Then the process is reversed: "As all had flowed in, so now all began to flow out, out from the Stone, out into the hands that held it . . ." (261). She becomes like the Stone. In order to return to the invisible world, it has passed through her body, and in so doing it takes her soul with it into the Unity and changes her body into something like its own outer appearance. But she is not dead, any more than the Stone is dead matter. She lies in Lord Arglay's house for nine months, after which she dies.

How are we to interpret this period of quiescence? To return to Chloe's likeness to the Virgin Mary, we see that in nine months a human being and God became one at the birth of Jesus. Chloe's loving offering of herself, supported by Lord Arglay, may be said to symbolize Love and the Law coming together to create a new understanding. At any rate, some form of new birth, we are led to believe, is what emerges at the end of the nine months, when Chloe's body dies. The reader can decide whether the new creation is Chloe's own joyous union with God in heaven, or a deeper understanding by Lord Arglay of the ways of God in this world. Perhaps it is both.

The Place of the Lion (1931)

In this novel Williams sees power, not as encased in one material object, such as a chalice or a stone, but as roaming the world. The great Ideas that form the nature of reality move about in the book in the symbolic form of beasts or other creatures.

The story is exciting. The Lion is first seen by Anthony Durrant and his friend Quentin Sabot, who find it in the garden of Mr. Berringer, who may have been attacked by it but is not injured; he remains unconscious. He, through his metaphysical studies, has called forth from the invisible world the forces that rule the visible, and they are now able to draw into themselves all their physical replicas. The Lion represents strength. The Snake, first seen by Dora Wilmot, is subtlety; and the Eagle, or wisdom, terrifies Damaris Tighe, with whom Anthony is in love. Damaris's father is so moved by Beauty in the form of an enormous Butterfly that he leaves off work to contemplate it and at last dies, absorbed into Beauty.

The story shows various reactions to this intrusion of the immortal Ideas into the world of matter. Quentin is driven nearly mad by his fear of the Lion, but Anthony, realizing that he himself must contain some essence of the Lion, stands firm against it through his inner control. He is aided by the Eagle. Thereafter he is able to rescue Damaris, whose misuse of her intellect has made her an object of the Eagle's attack. In a new humility she rescues Quentin, who is being pursued by Mr. Foster, a man who sought the Lion's power for his own use and is now brutalized, nearly an animal himself. In a similar way, Dora Wilmot, fascinated by the Serpent's ways, is in the end transformed into one. Richardson, a bookshop assistant, understands the nature of the beasts. His own passion is for union with God, and he sees the Unicorn, symbol of purity. In his desire to get rid of his body and see God, Richardson throws himself into the supernatural fire, symbol of the Phoenix (love) that has broken out in Berringer's house.

Terror increases as the Lion's strength draws more and more man-made things into itself—houses and telephone poles collapse and complete destruction seems inevitable. But Anthony realizes he must restore order. He calls the beasts and sends them back to the realm of primal energy from which they came.

Perhaps the first thing to attract the reader's notice in this novel is the importance of Ideas as vital, moving forces in our lives. As Anthony says to Quentin, it is more dangerous for a person to hate than to kill. Destructive thoughts produce violence.

The huge creatures that embody Ideas are seen by Williams as neutral forces, neither constructive nor destructive. Everything depends on how people react to them and recognize them as being also within themselves. They are the qualities that make up people, although they also exist in their own immaterial realm. Plato speaks of these Ideas in his *Phaedo* as the Archetypal Ideas that constitute true reality; what we see on earth, he says, are only faint replicas of the originals.

Presumably Berringer's occult experiments have opened a way for the immaterial Ideas to enter the world. Perhaps the success of his efforts, the actual appearance of the Lion, is too much for him; he remains unconscious throughout the story. But his house becomes the center from which the other Ideas emerge. Here Miss Wilmot sees the crowned Snake; and here the fire, or Phoenix, in the end consumes Berringer and Richardson.

There is a natural kinship between the ordinary animal we know, which Williams calls an image, and its immaterial Archetype. For this reason the Archetype draws back into itself all its images. A lioness that Anthony and Quentin see at the beginning of the story disappears into the Lion, and the zoo keepers look for her in vain. The Idea of Butterfly absorbs all other butterflies in the neighborhood; Anthony and Damaris's father watch and are amazed: "But—

a butterfly! It was a terrific, colossal butterfly, it looked as if it were two feet or more across from wing-tip to wing-tip. It was tinted and coloured with every conceivable brightness. . ." (40). As they watch, they see ordinary butterflies appearing and hurling themselves at the large one, which seems to be summoning them.

In a similar manner to this absorption of the butterflies, other creatures, and man himself, together with all his works, can be drawn into the Ideas now abroad in the world. That is the danger that Anthony understands. And this is what happens to Mr. Tighe; he becomes absorbed into the beauty of the Butterfly. Damaris, going into his room shortly before he dies, finds him changed; he is becoming transfigured, beautiful.

The other Ideas, moving into the world through Berringer's house, find their counterparts or images and begin to possess them. The Lion, symbol of strength, is seen by Anthony as "majestic, awful, complete, gazing directly in front of it, with august eyes." Its color is not yellow but gold, "with a terrific and ruddy mane covering its neck and shoulders" (38–9). The Serpent, or subtlety, is seen by most people, not directly, but as a rippling of the earth, a kind of minor earthquake. Its last appearance is to Richardson, who sees it take over the body of Miss Wilmot. In a description reminiscent of a passage in Dante's *Inferno*,[6] the author shows her body becoming like a snake's and then the Snake itself coming out. Richardson tries to pray to "the Maker and End of all created energies" (152), but as the Snake begins to move, he faints. Surely this world, in which the abstract Principles appear and take over their material counterparts, is more awesome than any Williams has elsewhere shown.

The Eagle, symbol of wisdom or the spiritual intellect, can be terrifying, as it it to Damaris in her selfish pretension to knowledge; or comforting, as it is to Anthony. When Quentin runs away in terror, Anthony is left alone with his resolution not to be afraid. High in the air he sees a bird that offers a kind of companionship, and a little later, when the Lion's strength seems about to overcome him, he is saved by experiencing a sensation of flying. The Eagle has taken him under its protection because he has already been seeking spiritual wisdom. Now he can begin to control the other

Ideas. For the Eagle is ruler of the others. It is called "that Wisdom which knew the rest and itself also, the very tradition of the Ideas and the Angelicals being but a feather dropped from its everlasting and effectual wing" (119).

Because he is being guided by the Eagle, Anthony finds the Horse, or Idea of speed, at his disposal when he needs to hurry to help Damaris. We see an ordinary cart horse being suddenly transfigured as it tears itself out of the harness: "Its white coat gleamed silver; it grew larger and burst the leather bands that held it; it tossed its head, and the absurd blinkers fell off . . . The horse made one final plunge and stood free" (123). Anthony leaps upon it and rides to Damaris; and Richardson, who is watching, sees what seem thousands of other horses, "a thundering army, riotous and untamed," going with them (124).

It is Richardson who sees the Unicorn as he stands at the open door of a Wesleyan chapel where a service is in progress. His eye is caught by a gleam of brightness that nearly blinds him, and then he sees it—"the Divine Unicorn gently sustaining itself in that obscure and remote settlement of the faithful" (143). Richardson's pure desire for union with God enables him to see the beautiful white creature that symbolizes purity. It is also called a symbol of "Return," or a return to man's original state of purity in Eden.

Damaris sees the Lamb, symbol of innocence, when, after her conversion, she goes to help Quentin and finds him running about in a field, with bleeding feet, pursued by the brutalized Mr. Foster. Damaris cannot stop the horrible pursuit, but she sees a single lamb moving slowly toward her. She goes to meet it, "and the innocence that sprang in her knew a greater innocence and harmlessness in it" (175). From this refuge, she calls persistently to Quentin to join her, and at last he does. Both are safe, for Foster is drawn away to meet the full force of the Lion. Harmlessness has turned aside all harm, or innocence has, contrary to all worldly beliefs to the contrary, absorbed and nullified cruelty.

All these Ideas or Principles, as Williams sees them, are contained in the Idea of love, symbolized by the Phoenix, the mythical bird that is consumed in fire and yet lives, constantly renewed. Its visible manifestation in the novel is Berringer's burning house. Richardson's suicide by plunging into the fire is a symbolic gesture. He gives himself to love and is outwardly destroyed, but he is certainly reborn in the invisible world, for love cannot be quenched. Perhaps the same fate is Berringer's.

We have seen that *The Place of the Lion* differs from some of the other novels in that it deals with energies or Ideas rather than with all these forces inherent in one object. Similarly, evil is now seen, not as action to obtain possession of an object, but as thought that somehow violates the Principle of love. Evil in *The Place of the Lion* takes the form of thought only.

Damaris Tighe, in her self-absorption and disregard of others, best illustrates the evil of thought that runs counter to love. She does not appear evil, being an attractive young lady who is diligently pursuing her research for a doctorate degree; and Anthony finds her adorable, though he is not blind to her faults. She accepts his devotion as a matter of course, not troubling much about returning his love. She resents anyone who interrupts her work or interferes with her schedule of study.

It is her attitude toward her scholarly work that proves to be, in the end, the means of her salvation from the hell of self-interest. She has thought of research only in terms of what it can do for her. The philosophers she studies can help her to achieve fame as an authority on medieval thought; it does not occur to her that their ideas have anything to do with life. When the Ideas take form as living creatures she at last begins to understand their power. Her first warning of danger comes as a very unpleasant smell; this has its source in her own self-concern, which is a moral corruption, a taint of death. Then wisdom in the form of the Eagle attacks her. In her terror as she tries to escape, she screams first for her father and then for Anthony. The room about her seems to melt away and she is in a kind of wilderness, trying to move through thick, muddy ground. There she sees Abelard, the philosopher she has been studying, become transformed from a joyous young man into a kind of corpse, which "croaked at her in answer to her own croakings, strange and meaningless words" (133). The croakings are, of course, what she has made, in her tight little research, of a philosophy that in itself was vital and good. She used philosophy for her own ends, just as she used her father and Anthony.

She is saved by Anthony's love, which is a type of Divine love rescuing her from the foul state of her inner life. As her vision of the boggy plain gives way to the normal room again, she is willing to listen to Anthony with a new humility.

The other two characters who sin through thought are Miss Wilmot, who turns into a snake, and Mr. Foster, who is destroyed by the Lion. Like Damaris, these two are dominantly self-centered. But they have no Anthony to serve as a channel for divine love and save them. As members of Berringer's study group, they are interested in the appearance of the Ideas in the world, but they seek not just to understand but to use the energies selfishly. Miss Wilmot, who has long admired subtlety, writes some letters of a scandalous nature to send anonymously in order to stir up trouble. Just after that she is transformed into the Snake; the subtlety that she sought now takes possession of her. Foster, having sought for the strength of the Lion, is overwhelmed by it. The change in him comes about gradually. He and Miss Wilmot make a sudden attack on Anthony, clawing at him like animals. Later Richardson meets Foster outside the Wesleyan chapel. Foster now seems to snarl as he speaks, and his voice is thick and blurred. Though keeping a roughly human shape, he becomes a beast of prey. His awful end is brought about by his own misguided seeking; but it is also explained by the fact that all the Ideas are finding and absorbing their counterparts.

Anthony is the hero of the novel. We see him as intellectually curious, open-minded, and imaginative. Like all of Williams's heroes and heroines, he does not dismiss something as impossible because it is out of the ordinary. Fantastic as the appearance of the Lion at first seems, Anthony is willing to consider the notion that the Lion and the other "angelicals," as the Ideas are sometimes called, have really taken shape in tangible form. When faced with adverse circumstances—Quentin's disappearance, Damaris's resistance to him, and the alarming threat of world destruction—Anthony resolves to act courageously, and "all the while to be quiet and steady, to remember that man was meant to control, to be lord of his own nature, to accept the authority that had been given to Adam over all manner of beasts. . . ." (75).

Thinking of the Lion and the Lamb, Anthony meditates on the need for a balance of both their qualities in man and in the world. Love, he reflects, is always the answer to perplexities. If the Ideas can be known as huge and violent by people who minimize the spirit, they can also be known in their proper shape through the power of love. And yet he knows that mankind is still not spiritually developed enough to see the Ideas through love alone; man cannot yet achieve that heavenly balance. So Anthony begins to see that the Ideas must return to their heavenly world—the as yet invisible realm where presumably the balance is perfectly kept and lions do lie down with lambs. He, Anthony, must call the Ideas by their names, as Adam did originally, and try to send them back to their place of origin: "Separately they had issued—strength divorced from innocence, fierceness from joy. They must go back together; somehow they must be called" (190).

He walks with Damaris out to the field where she rescued Quentin, not far from Berringer's house, which is still burning. As Damaris watches Anthony stride out across the field, the landscape seems to change, to become gigantic and primeval, an image of the original Paradise. And the burning house is transformed into a tree—the tree of life in the Garden of Eden, side by side with the tree of knowledge.[7] In this visionary country scene it is not surprising to hear Anthony call and be obeyed. But for a moment, as she watches, Damaris feels very much alone and neglected; her previous selfishness begins to assert itself: "Out of a sepulchre of death the old Damaris rushed up into the new; anger began to swell within her" (202). But she makes another surrender to the power of God and returns to her redeemed self. As Anthony begins to run back to her, she is aware of a reenactment of the departure of Adam and Eve from Paradise: "The earth shook under her; from the place of the trees there broke again the pillar of flame. . . The guard that protected earth was set again; the interposition of the Mercy veiled the destroying energies from the weakness of men" (205).

In this scene Williams has made a comment on the whole story of Adam and Eve—their easily falling a prey to sin and their expulsion from Eden, which was both inevitable and somehow right. The power of divine love, symbolized by the fire, is always in control, and its mercy protects man from ultimate reality until he is able to bear it.

To some readers the fate of the gentle young man named Richardson may seem inexplicable. Why does Richardson commit suicide by throwing himself into the fire, just before Anthony restores order in the world? His action is the result of a kind of thought that Williams elsewhere calls the Negative Way—a belief that since God is greater than any of the things He creates, we should devote ourselves to seeking God only, and any image or created thing is only a hindrance to finding that ultimate reality. The Negative Way is opposed to the Affirmative Way, which finds God in all His works; this is Anthony's way. Williams is sure that neither Way is superior; they are simply different approaches to God. What Anthony calls "the necessity" sends Richardson to his death in the fire; he wants to rid himself of all images and be aware only of spirit. Both young men, and all the characters in their several ways, are seeking for ultimate reality or God. Beneath all appearances, whether they are terrifying or joyful, there is God: this belief shines forth from every page of the book.

The Greater Trumps (1932)

In this novel we see a pack of cards, the mysterious Tarots, as an object of supernatural power. Williams did not invent the Tarots. They first appeared in Europe in the late fourteenth century and are considered to be the forerunners of modern playing cards.[8] But since their origin is not precisely known, and they have been used for centuries for fortune telling and other occult purposes, they form an admirable focus for a novel that deals with hidden meanings in ordinary events.

The plot centers on the desire of Henry Lee to own a set of Tarot cards belonging to Lothair Coningsby, the father of Henry's fiancée, Nancy. Henry invites Nancy, her father, and her father's sister Sybil to visit his grandfather, Aaron Lee, for the Christmas holidays.

Aaron possesses a set of golden images that correspond exactly to the pictures on Mr. Coningsby's Tarot cards. Convinced that they can discover deep secrets by a close comparison of the images and the cards, Aaron and Henry hope to buy or steal the cards. Unable to do so, they determine to kill Mr. Coningsby. Henry will use the magical properties of the cards to raise a storm on Christmas afternoon, when Mr. Coningsby will be taking a walk. He will, they think, never survive the fury of that storm. But things do not turn out as they plan. Sybil walks easily through the storm and rescues Coningsby. Nancy discovers Henry manipulating the cards and knocks them from his hand. Angry and terrified, Henry believes that without the cards he cannot stop the storm and they will all perish.

Despite her grief over Henry's treachery, Nancy is persuaded by Sybil to go to him and try to help him. She suggests that together they try to control the storm by means of the cards that remain and the golden images. In the room of the images Henry loses Nancy in the mist and knows spiritual desolation. She goes forward and turns back the power of the storm to the place of its origin.

Nancy then must face the wrath of Joanna, Aaron's mad sister, who believes herself to be the Egyptian goddess Isis. Her search for her child, Osiris, brings her to the room of the golden images, where she tries to "sacrifice" Nancy and thus "let out" the lost child. Nancy is saved by her father. The storm lessens, but a "living cloud" of enormous shapes of the Tarots pours down the stairs; it is dispersed by Sybil, who alone has remained unafraid. Two children are seen playing at Sybil's feet for a moment. The Tarot card named the Fool, which has been an actor in the whole drama, runs down the stairs. When he disappears, the mysterious golden light and the children also vanish. Joanna, Sybil says, is at last happy, for she believes Nancy to be her lost child, who is the Messiah.

Such is the bare outline of a story that gathers momentum as it goes on, like the supernatural storm that is its climax. Since the Tarot cards and the golden images are the cause and center of the storm, let us see exactly what they are.

There are four suits of ten cards each—called sceptres, swords, cups, and coins (or deniers), each with its King, Queen, Knight, and Knave. The four suits represent the four elements— earth, air, fire, and water. Then there are the twenty-one trump cards that give the novel its title: the Juggler, the Empress, the Emperor, the Pope, the Papess, the Chariot, the Lovers, the Hermit, Temperance, Fortitude, Justice, the Wheel of Fortune, the Hanged Man, Death, the Devil, the Falling Tower, the Star, the Moon, the Sun, the Last Judgment, and the Universe. These, plus the card that has no number and is called the Fool, make up the Greater Trumps.

The golden images are about three inches high and set out on a golden plate where they are in constant motion. They represent, as the cards do, a Juggler, Empress, Emperor, and the rest. When Henry tells Aaron about Mr. Coningsby's cards, Aaron suspects that they were made by the same person who, long ago, made the images, and that both cards and images were carried about in the vans of gypsies all over Europe. Aaron and Henry have gypsy origins.

Although Aaron now owns the images, he cannot understand why they move continuously as if in a strange kind of dance. Perhaps, he thinks, the meaning of the dance would be clear if the images could be joined again to their card replicas. In order to study images and cards together, he determines to have the Tarots.

But the conflict involving possession of the cards seems, as the story unfolds, less important than the symbolic meaning that both they and the images hold. The reader begins to understand that they symbolize a spiritual journey being undertaken by the characters.

In his book on the Tarot cards Alfred Douglas calls them symbols of man's journey to the recovery of his own soul, which he lost when he came to self-consciousness as a separate entity.[9] In *The Greater Trumps* we see the characters at the stage they have reached on this journey. Sybil Coningsby is the farthest along, Nancy makes some progress, and Lothair Coningsby and Henry Lee become dimly aware that there *is* a journey.

Throughout the novel Williams keeps us aware of the cards. They represent things in the everyday world and at the same time the spiritual significance of those things. For example, in the chapter entitled "The Chariot" the Coningsbys and Henry are driving to Aaron's house in the country, but at the same time they are on their way to greater enlightenment. A policeman directing traffic is both himself in a white coat and helmet and at the same time "the

Emperor of the Trumps, helmed . . . stretching out one sceptred arm" (55).

The power of the cards produces the action of the story. Since to Williams the supernatural is always present within the natural, the cards not only represent but can produce the four elements. As Henry tells Nancy, "When the hands of a man deal in a certain way with the cards, the living thing comes to exist" (50). He shows her how to use the coins, or deniers, to make earth; as she deals the cards in his way, she begins to feel a gritty substance between them, and soon there is a small heap of earth on the table. At the climax of the novel Henry shakes and beats the sceptres and the cups, symbols of water, to make the snowstorm.

The golden images are as strange as the cards. Anyone seeing their dance is fascinated by it: "Gently and continuously they went, immingling, unresting—as if to some complicated measure, and as if of their own volition" (28). This dance, to which the cards give a clue, is a visual representation of the movement of all matter, which, modern science tells us, is made up of constantly whirling atoms. And that movement is directed by the Creator, God. Each Tarot card vibrates "to the movements of its mightier golden original, as that in turn moved in correspondence to the movement of that full and separate centre of the created dance which it microcosmically symbolized" (153).

The only image in the dance that seems to most people not to move is the Fool, who moves so swiftly that he seems to stand still. He is pictured on the card as a young man in parti-colored dress, carrying a staff and a bag, with a lynx or young tiger by his side. He is bright-eyed and smiling: "the smile was so intense and rapt that those looking at it felt a quick motion of contempt—no sane man could be as happy as that" (20). He represents Christ and is called Fool "because mankind finds it [Christ's teaching] folly till it is known" (196). Nancy, in the room of the images, sees the Fool move because she has, by then, made some progress on her spiritual journey; but Sybil has seen the Fool move from the first time the images were shown to her.

As the story continues, Sybil realizes the true nature of the Fool. She finds him in the storm, taking care of her brother when she goes to search for him. Ahead of her is Coningsby's "crouching figure," half sunk into the snow; and as she runs toward it she sees the Fool, "another form, growing out of the driving snow—a tall figure that ran down on the white stairs of the flakes, and as it touched earth circled round the overwhelmed man" (126–27). Later, as she comforts Nancy when she is bewailing Henry's sending her father out to his death, Sybil says, "Do you suppose that storm can ever touch the Fool? . . . there's no figure anywhere in heaven or earth that can slip from that partner. They are all his for ever" (139).

Sybil is the chief character of the novel. Her name suggests the sibyls of ancient Greece, priestesses of the temple of the oracle, through whose mouths the god spoke. She is always peaceful in herself and does not get annoyed with other people as her brother does. Her complete reliance on the love that casts out fear is best shown in her rescuing Coningsby. Although no one else can stand upright in the terrible storm, she is sure she can walk without hindrance, "because it wasn't really she who was walking, it was Love, and naturally Love would be safe in his own storm" (125). Sybil's "unterrified and dominating serenity" (189) when the storm has swept into the house makes her a figure of whom the others stand a little in awe; and yet she remains believable and entirely human. Of all Williams's "good" characters—and he has a surprising number of them—she is perhaps the most memorable.

Sybil's greatest influence is on her niece Nancy, who gradually comes to understand that Love itself is greater than the individual love of one person for another. Nancy is young and romantically attached to Henry. Therefore she is astonished when her aunt tells her, in answer to her question, that she doesn't really love anyone. But at the church service on Christmas morning she becomes aware that her love for Henry is like that of Christ for the world; being in love, she is one with a power greater than herself. She sees everyone in a new light.

It is this new understanding that enables her to try to stop the storm. She has to fight her way through battering wind and snow to reach Henry, where he is creating the storm with the cards. After she has knocked them from his hands, she and Henry stagger back to the house where Henry secludes himself, leaving Nancy alone with her grief. She feels that her love is dead: Henry has tried to kill her father, and nothing can be the same between them again.

Sybil, when she has heard the whole story, tells Nancy that she must continue to love Henry, because the "mystery of Love" is not just "between those who like one another" (139). Nancy's job now, she says, is to make things right between her father and Henry. Nancy swallows her pride and resentment and makes the first move. When she gets to Henry's room, she finds she is given words to speak; she urges Henry to help her "see if the golden dancers can call back the staffs and the cups" (146), and thereby stop the storm. He agrees. Once she has given up her urge to despair, she makes progress along the spiritual path.

This spiritual power within her curbs the furious storm, which seems to her to be embodied in gigantic shapes of the staff cards. These shapes rush toward her and are turned back by the supernatural power in her hands. By the end of the day the snow has stopped falling.

Henry, always more self-centered than Nancy and longing for power, loses her in the mist that envelops them when they enter the room of the golden images. He has been thinking resentfully that he, not Nancy, ought to be leading the way in this venture. Now, when she is gone, his purgation begins. Unseen hands pinion him by his wrists and ankles. He is forced to stand immobile for what seems an endless stretch of time. His pride, which has been like a stone tower, is now being crumbled. At last, as he remembers Nancy's love, it topples down. But his ordeal is not yet over. As he begins to understand the depth of his own selfishness, he becomes hateful to himself. Such is his suffering that Mr. Coningsby, who stumbles upon him in the mist, sees him in the shape of the Hanged Man of the Tarot cards. By the end of the novel Henry's acceptance of his own wrongdoing makes him a more appealing character than before.

Mr. Coningsby, too, develops during the story. Naturally a peevish man given to self-pity, he braves not only the wrath of the mad Joanna but also the frightening mist that has poured out of the room of the images, in order to help Nancy. When he finds that Joanna has stretched Nancy out on a table and is tearing at her hand, trying to "let out" Osiris, he explodes in wrath and breaks Joanna's sinister spell.

Joanna is a bizarre figure, not taken very seriously by anyone, except perhaps by Sybil. She is, of course, more than a mad old woman. In her role as the seeker who never finds, she serves as a symbol of all the ignorant suffering of the world; she is the unsatisfied desire that does not know the healing, sufficient love of God. Near the end of the novel, as she is wailing the loss of her child, Nancy feels that the sound expresses the world's anguish, which she must somehow learn to transform, as Sybil does, by the power of love within her.

Sybil finds Joanna's lost child. In the last scene she becomes like the Sun on the Tarot card. A golden light seems to come from her figure, and some of those looking on see at her feet two children, "the company of the blessed," (228) playing peacefully.[10] Joanna runs toward Sybil, only to collapse at her feet. The magical children vanish, but Joanna looks up happily at Nancy, and Sybil explains that she has found her child: she believes Nancy to be Christ, whom all this time she has unknowingly sought.

In this last scene we see that the characters who have been (and to some extent remain) quite realistic, become stylized, counterparts of the golden images, each one performing his part in the great dance of the universe. The movement of matter itself is revealed briefly to the servant Amabel, who in the raging storm inside the house sees "the powers and princes of the dance." The whole house seems to have changed: "The walls, the stairs, the doors, the ceiling, were all alive. They were formed . . . of innumerable shapes, continuously shifting . . . Dark pillars of earth stood in the walls, and through them burning swords pierced, and huge old cups of pouring waters were emptied, and grey clubs were beaten" (221–22). Nancy, too, sees these elemental shapes, and then she sees Sybil stretch out her hand to quell the tumult.

Hands are important throughout the novel. Henry uses his to manipulate the cards and cause the storm; Nancy uses hers to turn it back. Sybil's hands are constantly at work, comforting, healing, blessing. And hands, as well as Tarot cards, seem to make up the substance of the supernatural storm within the house. There are invisible hands in the golden mist in the room of the images. Mr. Coningsby, struggling to find his way in the mist, feels his hands caught for a moment by a gentle, ghostly hand. Hands hold Henry immobile until he sees his own sin. These mysterious hands seem to represent the spiritual activity that is constantly going on in the world, though invisible. And human hands are seen to be the visible counterparts of the hidden forces at work, the "spiritual instruments of intention" (200) often used in ignorance of their real significance.

One expression of the good which is to be important in Williams's later novels appears in *The Greater Trumps* as a minor theme. This is the idea of exchange or substitution, someone bearing the evil or pain that oppresses someone else. So Nancy's love saves Henry, and when she herself needs help she is saved by her father. Coningsby is rescued from the storm by Sybil. Even Aaron, who thinks only of saving himself, is moved by seeing the magical children playing at Sybil's feet: ". . . Aaron saw them and was ashamed" (228). In this brief statement Williams is perhaps indicating Aaron's eventual salvation. For if the children represent the two halves of a divided self, the recognition of that division is the first step toward wholeness and peace.

Descent into Hell (1937)

The only one of Williams's novels that is not concerned with a striving for power, *Descent into Hell* is centered on three characters—Pauline Anstruther, who comes to know the supernatural life in the present world; an unnamed workman who commits suicide; and Laurence Wentworth, who chooses hell and descends into it.

Pauline, who lives with her elderly grandmother, Margaret Anstruther, is constantly anxious because she often sees an exact image of herself coming toward her and is terrified of meeting it. She confides in Peter Stanhope, the playwright, when she goes to take her part in a rehearsal of his play. He offers to "carry" her fear and does, so that she is no longer afraid. Pauline now wants to help someone else as she has been helped. Her chance comes when her grandmother sends her out one night to meet the dead workman who is seeking the road to London. In despair over his hopeless life, the workman had hanged himself from the scaffolding of an unfinished house. Now, having been reassured by Mrs. Anstruther that love still exists for him, he wants to return to London to accept the responsibility from which he formerly ran away.

When Pauline shows him the way, she simultaneously is aware of her long-dead ancestor who was burned for heresy. She sees him before his execution, in agony because of his fear of the fire. Pauline offers to "carry" his fear, and he goes to his death rejoicing in salvation. She is then aware of her double, her true self, a radiant being whom she need not avoid any more.

The house where the workman committed suicide belongs to Laurence Wentworth, a historian. Wentworth becomes a prey to jealousy, not only of a rival scholar, but also of a younger man, Hugh Prescott, who is approved by Adela, the young woman Wentworth is attracted to. He is consoled by a witch woman or succubus, who comes to him in the guise of Adela. He becomes a recluse and only reluctantly goes to inspect the uniforms he designed for use in Stanhope's play. Wentworth sees a fault in the uniforms but, in order to get away, he lies and says they are correct. He has a recurring dream of descending on a bright rope into a pit.

Wentworth's preoccupation with the succubus causes him to reject the real Adela when she comes to him for help; she is hysterical, having seen graves begin to open at the cemetery. In her illness that follows, Adela asks Pauline to seek help from Lily Sammile, a sinister woman who has at night become Wentworth's succubus. Pauline finds Mrs. Sammile at the cemetery, in the company of the restless dead. As she appears among them, they all vanish in a cloud of dust.

Wentworth, whose succubus has disappeared, goes to a dinner in honor of his rival. But his mind is no longer functioning. He has descended on the rope to the bottom of the pit; he is in hell.

Descent into Hell presents us with incredible happenings. There is some indication of the world that we know, but for the most part the novel deals with a visionary realm, one where the past and the present mingle, and the dead move about among the living.

One of the author's assumptions is that all time is one—that we are living in eternity and therefore are contemporaneous with everyone who has ever lived or will live. The reader is asked to try to imagine the world as seen by God: "In the place of the Omnipotence there is neither before nor after; there is only act" (102). Therefore Margaret Anstruther can have a vision of Laurence Wentworth and the dead workman standing side by side, looking out of the same window, though Wentworth's house was still only a scaffolding when the workman died. The past, as Williams sees it, goes on happening right along with the present. Thus Pauline, thinking of her ancestor while she is at the dress rehearsal, reflects on past and present: "He was not there; he was dead centuries since. If centuries meant anything; perhaps they didn't—perhaps everything was all at once . . . perhaps even now he burned, and she and her friends danced . . ." (150–51). As she begins to believe that all can exist side by side, she sees the possibility of her doing something to help her ancestor, but she struggles with her own disbelief, saying to her grandmother, "But how could he take it before I'd given it?"

Mrs. Anstruther's reply is, "Why do you talk of *before?* If you give, you give to It, and what does It care about *before?"* (158) Her "It" of course is God or Love, independent of time as man conceives it. Pauline's good intention will be received by God and used at the time of her ancestor John Struther's execution. We see John Struther come into existence on the road to London, just where the dead workman had been. But he is also standing in the place of execution; we see him in the past and present at once. The scene he saw is there, but mingled with it are the characters in the play being performed: "The heat scorched and blinded and choked him. He looked up through the smoke and flame . . . and saw . . . the face of his daughter's aeviternity. She only among all his children and descendants had run by a sacrifice of heart to ease and carry his agony" (173).

The contemporaneity of all times is essential to the novel. Pauline can reenter time at an earlier period and thus begin to grasp the truth of transcendency; the workman who has died some years before can be redeemed *now* by Mrs. Anstruther. Even more important, we are shown that exchange, or substituted love, first made clear by Christ's suffering for mankind, goes on eternally, independent of time.

Williams's idea of exchange, or of one person carrying another's burden—fear, anxiety, or pain—is touched upon in *The Greater Trumps* but not made prominent in his fiction until *Descent into Hell*. It is at one of the play rehearsals that Pauline tells Peter Stanhope about her fear of meeting her "double." After she leaves, he stays on, settling himself in his chair, and although watching the actors now and then, he gives his interior attention to Pauline's problem. He visualizes her walking home and deliberately opens himself to fear, "absorbing . . . the strangeness and the terror of that separate spiritual identity" (100). He does not try to determine whether the vision of her double is "real"; if she thinks it is, then it is so for her, and with utmost goodwill he substitutes himself for her in that situation. Pauline, as she goes home, finds herself forgetting to be afraid; suddenly she feels carefree for the first time in many years.

Gradually, then, Pauline comes to understand what Williams means by coinherence, which is the opposite of self-sufficiency: it is a constant interaction with other people, a living with and from them, giving and receiving help in the power of Christ.

As Pauline accepts this universe of coinherence, she is saved not only from her fear but from her former selfishness and isolation. A similar experience comes to the dead workman when, for the first time, he is offered love by another person. Margaret Anstruther sees his tortured face through her window, and she says "with a fresh spring of pure love, as if to Pauline or Phoebe or anyone: 'My dear, how tired you look!' " (121). Her concern communicates to him the love of God that releases him from fear and self-pity; he sees that joy is to be found in accepting himself and other people. Now he wants to follow the new way of joy and power: "He only moaned a little, a moan not quite of pain, but of intention and the first faint wellings of recognized obedience and love" (124). At this moment of turning away from his past futility, he is strengthened by God's own suffering. As the workman moans, Christ's agony is lived again: "But that moan was not only his. As if the sound released something greater than itself, another moan answered it . . . far off, beyond vision in the depths of all the worlds, a god, unamenable to death, awhile endured and died" (124–25). Thus the crucifixion of Christ is reenacted whenever someone like Mrs. Anstruther offers disinterested love to someone else.

From the moment when the workman's groan shudders through Battle Hill, strange things begin to happen. The sound seems to act as a catalytic power: the air becomes supernaturally bright; some people sicken; unquiet spirits leave their graves. Adela becomes more markedly self-centered and deceitful, but Pauline's joy increases.

This division of characters is between those who are willing, like Pauline, to accept facts, and those who insist on shrouding themselves in illusion. To Williams, the world of coinherence is the real, factual world that we can come to recognize; but we must work at it. Mrs. Anstruther who is an advanced soul, knows that there are "dream and fact" (or hell and heaven) in everything that happens to us; she thinks, "It is not enough to say that some experiences are drugs to the spirit; every experience . . . has a quality which has to be cast out by its other quality of perfection, expelled by healthy digestion into the sewers where the divine scavengers labour" (69). By "dream" she means living for self alone; "fact" is living in coinherence. The "quality of perfection" that can be found is the glorious fact that the universe is love. We must seek to uncover, even in the most adverse circumstances, the fact of God's presence.

The world of love and coinherence is what Williams calls sometimes the City, or the redeemed City, or the Republic, and sometimes Zion. Its opposite he calls Gomorrah, which is the city of illusion or self-deceit. The strange woman called Lily Sammile lives in Gomorrah; in the story nobody knows quite where she does live. She takes the form of Wentworth's succubus because she is really Lilith, who in Jewish folklore stood for an evil spirit or the shadowy first wife of Adam.[11]

Adela Hunt, egotistical and deceitful, is becoming familiar with Gomorrah. When she runs from the horror of the opening graves and seeks refuge in Wentworth's house, the deceit she has practiced turns back upon her. In a scene that is cold like treachery, Wentworth stands at the open window and turns her away, saying he does not know her. Looking past him into the room, she sees the succubus, who has a blank, dead face that is just like her own.

Adela, however, does not move so far on the way to hell as does Wentworth, whose insistence on having his own way shuts him off from the whole world. Originally a good scholar, he comes to deny intellect—he alters facts to make them agree with his pet interpretation. Next, he chooses anger and bitterness when his rival, Moffat, is given an honor; and when Adela prefers Hugh Prescott to himself, his resentment is such that he puts both young people out of his life. He enjoys the company of the succubus though his mind tells him she is false; but she is exactly like Adela, and without Adela's self-will. In a chapter called "Return to Eden" we see Wentworth walking with the succubus in a phantom garden, where mist is creeping over everything. Like another Adam, Wentworth succumbs to the temptation to think himself godlike. Another step downward to hell comes when he inspects the uniforms of the guard in Stanhope's play. He knows instantly that the shoulder knots are wrong. They could easily be corrected by his housekeeper, but giving the instructions would be a bother and would mean his losing time with the phantom Adela. He lies and says the uniforms are correct.

After that, his end is inevitable. By the time the real Adela comes to him for help, his choice of hell is unrestricted by any gleam of conscience or any normal pity. He has chosen self and excluded the world. The intelligence that he has outraged dwindles in him. In the last painful scene where he sits at the banquet table in London, he can no longer recognize faces or voices. He feels himself "looking up an avenue of nothingness" (221), and then even the sounds cease, and he is drawn down into a void of idiocy.

Wentworth's fate is so horrible, and so logical, that it makes a greater impact on the reader than does Pauline's joy. But the author's point is unmistakable: to refuse coinherence is to be in hell, and to accept it is a state of heaven.

The recurring themes of the novel are as carefully worked out as motifs in a symphony. Williams is not writing hastily, as he sometimes seems to be in earlier novels. He is now at the height of his power, showing a skill and subtlety not attained before. For example, the theme of meeting oneself occurs not only in the story of Pauline but also in that of the workman and of Adela. Both the workman and Wentworth use a rope to enter a kingdom of death. There are many images of light and dark, and light is often associated with the image of rock, which symbolizes something eternal, the fact of God or the moral order. In contrast, the images of Gomorrah are all soft, melting, shadowy ones. Light seems to flash through the novel, penetrating into dark places and revealing their sterility and nothingness, for, as we have seen in earlier works, Williams believes in the fundamentral goodness, or light, of the universe. His juxtaposition of the supernatural with the ordinary is seen in the "intolerably bright" (136) summer air which is noticed on the Hill after the workman's agony has been taken up into Christ's crucifixion. Peter Stanhope calls the new brightness a power "that increases everything that is, and decreases everything that isn't" (137).

All Hallows' Eve (1945)

In this, his last novel, Williams is again concerned with death and judgement. The subject matter is natural, when we consider that the book appeared in the last year of World War II and three months before Williams's own death. Unable to take part in the war himself, he suffered keenly in knowing that so many others were dying.[12] People in England expected to be bombed or invaded at any moment. Life was precarious. It is not surprising, therefore, to find that the two young women at the center of the novel, Lester Furnival and Evelyn Mercer, are dead when the story opens.

The forces of good are those of Lester, who learns to forgive; her husband Richard, who has several glimpses of her soon after her death; Richard's friend Jonathan Drayton, an artist, and Jonathan's fiancée, Betty Wallingford.

Evelyn allies herself with evil forces. Betty's mother, Lady Wallingford, has for years been the mistress of Simon the Clerk, a magician who sets up as a religious leader and hopes eventually to rule the world. Betty was conceived with the express purpose of making her Simon's tool and messenger in his occult work. One of his first actions in the story is to put Betty into a trance and send her soul into the future to gather news of his attempted world domination.

While Betty is in the streets of the other world, she calls to Jonathan, who, being in the present time, does not hear her. But Lester and Evelyn do. They knew Betty at school, where Evelyn delighted to torment her. Now she tries to do so again, but Betty returns to her body and enters the house. Lester follows her and finds Simon trying a more drastic experiment on Betty, to kill her body and keep her soul barely alive, in complete subjection to him. Lester, unseen by Simon, calls out to Betty to offer help, and the evil spell is broken.

Simon realizes Lester has frustrated his plans and seeks to control her by confining her soul with that of Evelyn in a new body, a magical image of a dwarf woman. Evelyn welcomes the body; Lester endures it as a temporary necessity. She guides the body to Jonathan's studio, where she is able to speak in her own voice to Richard, Jonathan, and Betty. The three friends and the dwarf drive to Simon's hall, where Simon makes a last attempt to kill Betty by piercing an image of her with a needle. He fails because it is All Hallows' Eve, a time when the power of God is especially evident. Simon's magic weakens: all his past works return to him and disintegrate before him. Those he has healed become ill again and he himself perishes, dissolving in the rain. Momentarily, Lester's and Evelyn's souls, released from the dwarf body, stand in their earthly forms, and Lester and Betty try again to turn Evelyn aside from her hellish path. But she rushes in fancied triumph out of the window. Lester vanishes from the sight of her friends; and Betty, with the remainder of a supernatural energy that has been lent her, goes about healing the diseases of Simon's victims.

Even more strikingly than in *Descent into Hell,* Williams shows in *All Hallows' Eve* his belief that the soul continues its development after death. Death to him is not a solution to all problems or an immediate release into heaven. Rather, a person is still confronted with decisions and choices. Nothing is really easier; indeed, the loss of a body is, in some ways, rather hampering.

He pictures the place to which the dead first go as a kind of neutral place—quiet, lit with a faint light, insubstantial and yet, at first, just like what they had known when living. They can see things and people, especially ones that had meant something to them in life, but everything that was solid on earth—their bodies, houses, other people—is now shadowy, subject to fading away unless by their own soul's activity they can reestablish it in a new way, the way of love or heaven. If they deny love and insist on evil, they become progressively more insubstantial. Williams thinks of solidity as a quality of good or heaven.

The souls of the dead girls, Lester and Evelyn, retain for a time the appearance that the body had on earth. Lester finds herself in what seems an empty city; she feels vague and helpless and begins to cry, aware of tears on her face. She looks around for her handbag, to find a handkerchief, but the bag is not there. When a figure that seems to be Richard approaches her and then fades away, she at last realizes she is dead. But she seems to have a body—Richard has recognized her.

The body as Williams thinks of it, is essential to the soul, a vital part of it, from which the soul is temporarily separated at death. The body is the soul made visible. The fact that her body can no longer be seen (except in rare moments by people like Richard and Betty, who love her) has nothing to do with the reality of Lester's soul. It will eventually find a way to be reunited with the body, and that reunion will be heaven.

When Betty goes out, under Simon the Clerk's magic spell, to read newspapers for him in the future, she goes in a "seeming body" like those of Lester and Evelyn. But she will return to her real body, as Lester and Evelyn cannot do: "[Betty's] actual body lay now crouched in the porch of the house, unconscious, waiting her return" (73).

Lester and Evelyn illustrate the choices of heaven or hell. Lester chooses the way of reconciliation and love and finds things becoming more substantial. Evelyn, who hates everyone and seeks only her own comfort, finds her apparent body becoming light, floating, and painfully insubstantial. During the course of the novel Lester and Evelyn are in the shadowy realm where choice is made, and by the end they are going on their separate ways to experience what they have chosen.

They are related as they had been in life—casual friends who already in life had begun to make choices. Lester finds herself, just after death, having to listen to Evelyn's trivial chatter because in life she had been too lazy to break away from an acquaintanceship she had not really approved of. Now, in death, they sit on an empty bench in the park, and Lester endures Evelyn's whimpering because she pities her and because they had often been together in life. She hates having Evelyn clutch her arm in fear, but she allows it because "her heart acknowledged a debt" (21).

Lester also thinks of her frequent anger against Richard, her husband. They had often quarreled bitterly, but they really loved each other; and at first she is miserable, thinking she has died without having his forgiveness. But then she reflects that, as in her relation with Evelyn, the past must be accepted, and where she had been wrong she must now make amends. This twilight time after death becomes for Lester an experience of purgatory.

It is her will toward the good that causes her to take a stand against Evelyn's wish to torment Betty. Recalling the many times at school when she had not helped Betty, she now resolutely follows her up the steps and into the Wallingford house. Inside, she learns what forgiveness really is—not just words one says while still cherishing a grudge, but a selfless love that does not want to remember the injury. Betty forgives Lester so lovingly and happily that Lester begins to get a glimpse of the life of coinherence; she sees that forgiveness must be the sustenance, the bread and wine, of the new life.

In this way Lester is enabled to perform the act of substitution that ensures her progress, her becoming "solid" in good. She can now offer to help Betty when Simon comes in, even though she is not sure what form her help can take. She only knows that Betty, though apparently asleep, is in great distress, and she calls out, unheard by Simon or Lady Wallingford, "Betty, if you want me I'm here" (142). Immediately she finds a deathly light creeping up her body. Then she is also aware of her body resting on a strong support, like a wooden frame. She stretches out her arms on it and feels secure. In this symbol of Christ's cross, Williams is indicating that, as happened to the workman in *Descent into Hell*, the slightest attempt of a person (Margaret Anstruther in that novel, Lester in this) to help someone else is reinforced by the substitution made by Christ for the world. After Lester's selfless offer of help, all the powers of good are strengthened, and Simon becomes progressively less effective.

It will be noted that in *All Hallows' Eve,* as in *Descent into Hell,* the sins that are repented of are not, for the most part, overt acts; they are sins of thought. The workman, in *Descent,* has moments of bitter feeling against those who have wronged him; Lester has, through indifference, failed to give encouragement to a classmate who was bullied. Most people, Williams believes, are not spectacular sinners; but we all fail in love and humility. His novels deal with those common failings and impurities of thought that, if persisted in, become "hellish."

Evelyn, who chooses the downward path, is not seen as evil at first. She is merely boring, childishly self-centered, and hostile to other people. She is sure that people are always unfair to her. Her fear for her own safety and her distrust of everyone are evident in her thoughts when Lester enters the Wallingford house to help Betty. Evelyn dares not follow her: "She hated the victim of her torment, but to be alone with her in that dark solid house . . . was not at all agreeable. As for Lester, she hated Lester too" (125). As she stands there on the doorstep, "The kind of rage that was in her was the eager stirring of the second death" (85). Evelyn, that is, becomes fixed in hate and malice; these terrible qualities are becoming immortal in her. She refuses to grow, and she wants to express herself just as she did in life; therefore, she feels an urgent need for another earthly body and welcomes the dwarf body that Simon makes. When she speaks from this dwarf body to Betty, we are shocked by her refusal to change. She says plaintively, "No-one . . . cares about me. I don't expect much. I don't ask for much. I only want you, Betty . . . I only want to see you cry . . ." (208).

The contrast between Lester and Evelyn is a contrast between two kinds of life. Those who aspire toward coinherence find that it can be attained, at least for a while, whether they are living or dead. Betty, when she enters the future to carry out Simon's instructions, enters a happy state, a joyous new consciousness. Richard, Lester's husband, begins to sense the life of coinherence when he first sees Lester after her death. His understanding of it is strengthened when he sees a painting his artist friend, Jonathan, has made of the City, full of light. Although the light in the picture is almost unbearable, he feels "despite himself, by his sight of Lester, some way initiated into that spiritual world" (133). When Lester tells him, near the end, that hereafter she will no longer be visible to him, he feels despairingly that the new life has gone. But, "He was as yet ignorant of the fact that this was one method of its becoming actual" (210). Lester must disappear before Richard can find the life of coinherence with other people and live always in love. Lester's going away is perhaps comparable to Christ's ascension so that the Holy Spirit could come to strengthen his disciples.

Lester goes, we are to believe, to the City that Jonathan, by his artist's intuition, had painted, the City that always exists, side by side with the London that people call "real." Already she has caught a glimpse of it, a "glowing and glimmering" (167) place. Since both Lester, who is dead, and Betty, who is living, can begin to know the "pure freshness of joy" (117) of this City, we realize that Williams is imagining its attainment as "not a journey in space, but in perception and response; not a removal but a modulation."[13] Just as sin is a turning away from love in one's thoughts, so redemption is a willing response to love, or God. The City can be entered at any time.

The forces working against the appearance of the City are represented by Simon the Clerk. Simon is self-centered, ruthless, and greedy for power. Like Considine in *Shadows of Ecstasy*, he has lived for centuries, for evil never dies. Simon attempts to dominate both the visible and the invisible worlds—the visible by means of magical "doubles" of himself in Russia and China, and himself in England; the unseen world by means of Betty, who can proclaim his rulership there.

Simon has deliberately chosen exile from God. To balance his unwillingness to return to loving obedience, all his evil works return to him when his schemes are frustrated by the power of love. The most appalling return is that of the two false Simons, two "slightly sinister caricatures" (232) of himself. When Simon sees them, he panics, for he realizes he cannot unmake them; he would be destroying himself. Confused by their appearance and by the brilliant rose-colored light around him and the rain driving into the hall, he becomes powerless.

Simon's end and Lester's "ascension" take place on All Hallows' Eve, the night before All Saints Day, when Williams believes that the power of God is most vividly manifested. He uses the word *hallows,* both here and in his poetry, to mean the "visible proofs" of Christ's love,[14] the evidence of His presence. So, in the last climactic scene of the novel, the rose-colored rain is one of the hallows. On the material level, it seems only "October closing in a deluge" (218), but spiritually the rain is "the vigil of the saints . . . innumerably active in the City" (218). This fresh rain, flashing in an unearthly light around all the characters assembled in the hall, literally dissolves Simon and all his evil. He is absorbed into a supernatural rose of love, which to him can only mean violence, antipathy, and extinction.

Chapter Four
The Poetry

Although Charles Williams wrote several volumes of verse before 1938, when *Taliessin through Logres* appeared, the early poems are imitative in style and would be little read if it were not for the Taliessin poems—which include also *The Region of the Summer Stars* (1944)—on which his reputation as a poet must finally depend. Lovers of Williams's work will always seek out the early verse and find in it some of his favorite themes and even early drafts of the more mature poems, but the present study will concentrate on the poetry that seemed to him, as it does to present-day critics, most significant.

The World of the Poetry

Taliessin through Logres and *The Region of the Summer Stars* have as their background the materials of romances concerning King Arthur, the half-mythical, early British ruler who has been the subject of other literary works, notably Sir Thomas Malory's *Morte d'Arthur* and Lord Tennyson's *Idylls of the King*. Taliessin is Arthur's court poet, but, more widely, he represents the poetic imagination in general; it is through Taliessin's eyes that the events and moods of the poems are seen. Logres is the ancient name for Britain. Williams treated some of the themes of his poems in an unfinished book called *The Figure of Arthur.*[1]

His basic source for the poems was Malory's long narrative of King Arthur's victory over other warring chieftains in early Britain and his establishment of a kingdom whose capital is Camelot. Where Malory gives lengthy accounts of the knights who come to Arthur's court and the various exploits they undertake, Williams puts his chief emphasis on Sir Galahad and the coming of the Holy Grail to Logres. The love of Sir Lancelot for King Arthur's wife, Guin-evere, is given its place in Williams's cycle of poems, but it is not so important there as in Tennyson's *Idylls*. To Williams, the Grail is of supreme interest. It was the cup that Christ used at his last supper with his disciples before he was arrested, and in which a friend caught drops of his blood as he hung on the cross. We recall the awe that the Grail inspires in Williams's novel, *War in Heaven*, and the miraculous powers it has in that tale. In the poems it becomes a symbol of the religion that is so greatly needed in secular society.

Just as in the novels, where the chalice *(War in Heaven)*, the Stone *(Many Dimensions)*, and the pack of Tarot cards *(The Greater Trumps)* carry with them a sense of joy but also of discipline, so the Grail in the poetry is a real but elusive presence uplifting people to a more selfless way of life. But in Logres its values are disregarded by the self-indulgent and selfish. The religious dimension is lost sight of in a universe torn by conflict.

The universe of the poems is sixth-century Europe, where the historical Arthur might have lived. Logres is a province ("theme") of the Byzantine Empire, the seat of the Roman Empire after the provincial tribes had captured Rome. Williams chose Byzantium as a symbol of wholeness, a perfect balance of body and soul—possibly because under Byzantine rule the church and secular society were more nearly unified than at any other period of history.

The Empire, as Williams sees it, is not only a unified community but also a symbol of the "whole nature of man,"[2] including, of course, his body. For the first edition of *Taliessin through Logres*, a friend of Williams's drew a map of Europe in the form of a woman's body, the parts of which are frequently mentioned in the poems. Logres is the woman's head; her buttocks (Caucasia) represent the natural, physical side of the human being; and her hands are at Rome, where the Pope performs with his hands the Eucharist, in which body and soul are of equal importance and are seen as one in Christ.

In this Empire, where God (the Emperor) is so active, and the invisible world constantly interacts with the visible, it is not too much to expect the second coming of Christ. Taliessin tells of hap-

penings in Logres, where the Holy Grail is seen, and Galahad, who
represents the capacity of man for Christ, appears at King Arthur's
court. But the hope of the second coming is frustrated. Although
in the peaceful kingdom established by Arthur there has grown to
be, among Taliessin and his friends, an understanding of Christ's
life within their own, there have also been elements of discord.
Lancelot, Arthur's friend, falls in love with Queen Guinevere. Arthur
himself, a symbol of the mind of man, sees the good of the kingdom
as fulfilling his own ideas. He has also, though a good man, once
unknowingly committed incest with his half-sister Morgause, and
thus begotten Mordred, who is to betray him. In time war breaks
out between Arthur and Lancelot, and the Holy Grail withdraws.
The second coming of Christ is not yet to be.

Such is the story behind the poems and referred to obliquely in
them. But there are other places in Williams's myth with which
we become acquainted. Outside the Empire but never quite out of
sight is Hell, called P'o-lu, the slimy region of the Emperor without
intelligence (the headless Emperor) and the pool of octopi. At the
western border of Logres is the mysterious sea-wood called Broceliande, a numinous region "between nature and eternity"[3] where the
creation of nature and man is continually taking place. It can be
thought of as the subconscious element in man and is called "the
place of making." It is "primeval and wild, the part of the mind
from which images are derived,"[4] and is both dangerous and exciting. In Broceliande man becomes aware of his infinite potentialities.

Then there are also the two holy cities. Caerleon is the place
where King Arthur is crowned; it is the seat of the Primate of
England and so corresponds to Canterbury today. Sarras, the other
city, is the spiritual place or city of the soul, to which Galahad sails
when the kingdom is breaking up. There he dies, like the Archdeacon in *War in Heaven*, during a celebration of the Eucharist.
Sarras is not on a map, for each person knows where he or she finds
it.

Within Broceliande is the city of Carbonek, where the Grail and
the sacred lance, which pierced Christ's side when he was crucified,
are guarded by King Pelles and his daughter Helayne. Malory tells
the story of how Balin, a fierce knight of Arthur's court, comes to

Carbonek. A dispute arises between Balin's followers and the servants of Pelles; Balin has no weapon on him, and he seizes the sacred lance and wounds Pelles. The blow that he strikes is called the "dolorous blow" and becomes a symbol in Williams of the fall of man, to be seen reflected in the sins of Arthur, Lancelot, and Guinevere. The wound given to Pelles does not heal; he lies waiting for a deliverer, who is to be Galahad, the only one whe can restore him to health. This action of Galahad shows that man's capacity for good can restore him to a right relationship to God.

The poems are full of symbols, strange names, and intricate relationships. Are they worth the effort of puzzling out? Opening either book at random, a casual reader is bewildered. To add to his difficulty, the poems do not tell a story. The story, as sketched above, is there, but only implied. Most of the poems deal with individual characters or with ideas about the relationships of people at Arthur's court. They are not a consecutive narrative, but rather, "Each poem is a small window onto a large world."[5]

Gradually, as we read, keeping in mind Williams's views and images in the novels and plays, the poems become clearer and send the mind out and out into wider horizons of thought and imagination. John Heath-Stubbs compares the whole body of the poetry to a cathedral filled with Byzantine mosaics:

At first our eyes are bewildered by the ranks upon ranks of stiff and apparently forbidding figures—saints and angels, virgins, martyrs, emperors and soldiers. Then gradually, we become conscious of the significance of the whole design, and are overpowered by the splendour of gold and porphyry, and inlaid glass.[6]

In both the poems and the mosaics there is a lack of ordinary perspective; the world we know is disregarded for the sake of meaning and pattern. And the brilliant colors and use of gold are characteristic of both.

The world of Williams's poetry is our ordinary world—that of love, sex, work, money, self-centeredness—but seen from other points of view, and thus it throws light on our everyday experiences and gives them more significance.

Taliessin's Vision for Logres

Let us turn, then, to the poems of the first volume, *Taliessin through Logres*. In a short, rather enigmatic "Prelude" the whole story of Logres is given in outline: first, we see the Empire established in the world and in individual man, meaning unfallen man living in a social order or Empire in which body and spirit (Caucasia and Carbonek) can, in ordinary living (Camelot), show forth the love and light of God. All places in the Empire (or all aspects of man) can accept and reveal the perfect order of God, the "diagram of the glory." Logres is seen as a part of the Empire.

Then, in section II of the poem, we see Logres failing in its mission, its rulers trying to govern with the mind alone instead of the whole being. We see Arthur breaking "the seals of the saints," ignoring the Pope's command that he refrain from war with Lancelot. For this private quarrel, the Round Table is split apart; as a symbol of unity in Logres it is destroyed—"the chairs . . . reeled." Thereafter, the unity of the whole Empire begins to give way, as Christianity is attacked by Mohammedans, and men in their selfishness try to hide from God, the "lord of charity." Yet even in this chaos Galahad has been born to show that God's mercy does not cease. Section III pictures the state of the world when it has fallen to the Moslems. Since Moslems deny the sanctity of the body and do not believe that God became incarnate, Caucasia, symbol of the body, falls into disgrace. Man loses the unity he had in Section I of the poem; body is divorced from spirit, and "the glory of substantial being" is lost.

There follows a quite different kind of poem, "Taliessin's Return to Logres." Here the poet is the central character, through whose eyes the tale of Logres is unfolded. Brought up as a pagan, Taliessin has been on a journey to Byzantium to find out about Christian belief and life. Now he returns home to Wales and then makes his way to King Arthur's camp, to try to work for the Christian king in his campaign to bring religion and order to his new kingdom.

The way that Taliessin takes is exciting and beautiful, but rather fearsome. As he rides through the woods, the creaking of the oaks in the wind echoes the creaking of the ship's mast that had been in his ears on the voyage. All is very dark, until suddenly a flashing of falling stars reminds him of the golden sickle used in rites of the Druids, the priests and seers of ancient Britain.

He rides on, thinking of his desire to be a poet (his harp, symbol of the poetic imagination, hangs on his back) and also of the dangers of the wood he is in. This is Broceliande, the strange, primeval forest. Taliessin thinks of how Comus, Circe's son, through his sorcery changed travellers into people with beasts' faces.[7] He thinks of a madman with a beast's face running through the wood and of "spectral shapes" standing near him "propped against trees."

But remembering his poetry, he takes courage, especially when he sees a sickle moon rise. It might be the Druid sickle again, but it also seems to him as if a golden arm had been stretched out and a hand had "caught the hallows," the sacred symbols of Christ's presence made visible to man. Elsewhere Williams named the three "hallows" as the Grail, the lance that pierced Christ's side as He hung on the cross, and the crown of thorns that He wore. In this poem they are not seen specifically but are felt as powerful forces: when the first of them falls like a star, the poet's feeling of panic vanishes; when the second falls, he knows that he can survive the dangers of Broceliande; and when the third appears, he finds himself arriving at Arthur's camp. He enters confidently the place where he feels he belongs.

This brief explanation of the poem gives no real idea of its beauty and vigor. It shows a vivid response to both ordinary and extraordinary experience. It moves lightly, quickly, its rhyme never obtrusive but giving a delicate music, its short lines carrying the reader forward with Taliessin. Imagery of dark and light suggests the acceptance of all of life. Nothing is to be denied—neither the shooting stars in the night sky nor the creaking darkness of the supernatural wood. And there is more light than darkness. In the last stanza the poet sees "a Druid light / burn through the Druid hills" and at the same moment he hears at the camp "the running of flame," which suggests both the vitality of the life he is entering and the warm human welcome that awaits him.

"The Vision of the Empire" tells us what Taliessin learned in Byzantium. There he was given a vision of what creation was meant to be—an organic whole, in which all parts coinhere in one another.

This whole he has seen in the form of a human body, the only way that we all experience how to live.

In the first section of the poem we see the Empire in its original, unfallen state, with all the parts singing in unison, and the "logothetes," angels or word-bearers, running down the porphyry stair between heaven and earth, bearing the Acts, or laws of love, from the Emperor. Taliessin has had an audience with the Emperor, or a vision of God, and he is now about to return to the ordinary world, the "place of images" (what we can grasp of eternal ideas). He stands at the harbor of Byzantium, the Golden Horn, aware of all the divine activity throughout the Empire.

Looking out, he sees first Caucasia, the physical nature of man. This is the foundation of our life and "the rounded bottom of the Emperor's glory." He sees the ranged peaks of Caucasia—Sinai, where Moses received God's law; Ararat, where Noah's ark rested; and Elburz, snow-covered, representing "true physical glory."[8] He sees also the young people of Caucasia dancing in the sunshine, showing the innocent sensual pleasures that are part of the intended harmony of man's nature.

He then looks northwest to Logres, the province that is the head of the organic body. There is Merlin, looking into the future, seeing that Camelot, Arthur's capital, is intended to be joined to Carbonek, the city of the soul. Merlin sees also the knight Percivale and his imagination of a union of soul and body; but Taliessin is aware that the union is threatened by Lancelot's lion, or heraldic crest, near Guinevere.

Gaul, the next province or theme, is the place of understanding. Williams had it pictured on the diagram as the breasts, the place where man is nourished by "the milk of doctrine." As C. S. Lewis notes, Gaul is the part of Europe that saw the rise of scholastic philosophy in the university of Paris in the Middle Ages.[9] Taliessin, looking at Gaul, feels that his visit to Byzantium has given him a knowledge of Christianity that he can take back to Logres.

He then considers the hands, located at Rome. Hands have built the Roman roads and bridges. But it was also hands that fashioned "iron nails" that, more powerful than fingernails, were used in the crucifixion of Christ. Yet, after Christ's "seed-springing surrender" (giving up self, from which sprang man's salvation), the hands of a heathen priesthood became those of Christian priests. This stanza reaches its climax with Taliessin's thought of the sacrament of the Eucharist performed by the Pope.

The consideration of the Pope leads in the next stanza to the question, why is the painful sacrifice being reenacted by the Pope? In "what was the crossing of the will of the Emperor?" the implied question is, why, in the harmonious Empire described earlier in the poem, did Christ have to suffer? The answer is given in an account of the Fall of Adam and Eve, whom Williams as usual calls "the Adam," using the singular word as having a plural meaning of man and woman.

The significance of this account is best seen in Williams's *He Came Down from Heaven*, chapter 2, which retells the story of Adam and Eve. Briefly, his idea is that they, experiencing only joy and peace in the Garden of Eden, felt there must be something more— the opposite of bliss—and they determined to know this other thing, evil, as God knew it. In "The Vision of the Empire" Williams suggests their temptation by the serpent in the circling movement of their thought:

> softly their thought twined to its end,
> crying: *O parent, O forkèd friend,*
> *am I not too long meanly retired*
> *in the poor space of joy's single dimension?*

They climb the tree of the Knowledge of Good and Evil and look out over a "secluded vision of battle in the law." It is secluded because even with their new knowledge they cannot see the whole pattern. But they see enough to feel terror. Being finite, they cannot know evil merely as a possibility, as God does. They have to know it by experience: therefore the tree they are on begins to wither, and they feel it twisting and their bodies twisting on it, in a terrible kind of crucifixion. In their distorted vision there are now two things—good versus evil—where actually only the one good exists: "Joints cramped; a double entity / spewed and struggled, good against good."

Another aspect of their suffering is the way they now see God, the Emperor, as a lonely figure walking in the night. Behind him creeps a loathsome object, "a white pulsing shape" which appears to be what the Adam had spewed forth, their "rejection of salvation." The white shape might also have a sexual meaning as "the semen, the sexual centre of life undirected by love or reason."[10] In several places the sexual aspects of the Fall are implied; the Adam no longer have love to control their lust.

The next section is full of unpleasant negative images; we see the results of the Fall in pictures of stagnation, lack of movement. A "single galley," perhaps man's spirit, now uncertain of its way, "hardly moves." The becalmed shipmen hear the harsh cries of birds and feel hot ashes raining down on them "from unseen volcanoes."

Even more dismaying is the fact that intelligence has now vanished. In another verse P'o-lu, or Hell, is pictured where a headless emperor walks through stagnant, phosphorescent water, wearing a crimson cope that parodies "the flush on the mounds of Caucasia." He is surrounded by octopi, lifting and waving hideously in the water. All the "substantial instruments of being" are lost, and only sensation is valued; his penis, gleaming phosphorescent, is perhaps singled out because it shows how sex has become overvalued and degraded.

The last section of the poem is a song of praise. Having just seen the body changed and shamed by the Fall, we are now reminded that body and soul were redeemed by Christ, and so a song rises through all of Byzantium. It is in the style of the Benedicite: every part of the human body and the geographical body is commanded to bless and praise God. So Taliessin's vision ends in an anthem of triumph.

Logres is Established

Now that Taliessin has returned to Logres with some understanding of what the country might become, the next step is to take practical action. Things are in disorder, with warring factions within and piratical marauders without. A leader is desperately needed, and in "The Calling of Arthur" and the two poems following, we see Arthur's rule begin.

He is called to the work by Merlin the wizard, who also symbolizes Time. Like a prophet of old—unkempt, "wolfish," he meets Arthur on the road and makes specific demands. From the second stanza until the last, the poem consists of Merlin's description of the chaos in the kingdom and the need for Arthur to act. The urgency of his message is increased by the intense cold of the day, indicated in staccato lines; the wind takes one's breath away—speech must be brief:

> Bold stood Arthur; the snow beat; Merlin spoke:
> Now am I Camelot; now am I to be builded.
> King Cradlemas sits by Thames; a mask o'ergilded
> covers his wrinkled face, all but one eye.

Cradlemas is Williams's symbol for the eleven kings that, in Malory, Arthur had to overcome in order to rule in Logres. The king's degeneracy is shown by the gold mask and his monocle made of an emerald, like Nero's. Cradlemas, who keeps himself apart from the people, is unaware that some of them, like Bors, are working quietly to overthrow him. But they need a leader. Lancelot is coming from Gaul with troops, and it is time for Arthur to act. When he does so, changes in Logres are described like sharp hammer blows.

The effectiveness of the poem comes from contrast: the soft effeminacy of King Cradlemas and the harshness of Merlin; the luxury of the king's life and the relentless cold that oppresses the people:

> The waste of snow covers the waste of thorn;
> on the waste of hovels snow falls from a dreary sky;
> mallet and scythe are silent; the children die.

There is contrast, too, between Arthur's youth and vigor and the old king's immobility and withering mind. It is as if a half-dead branch on a tree is broken off, and new life springs.

Having settled the internal affairs of his kingdom, Arthur now must defend it against marauders from without. In "Mount Badon" we see a host of pirates attacking the city wall; and within, Arthur's forces are fighting on a central plain, now gaining on the enemy, now losing and falling back.

Taliessin, although he is the king's poet, is also his "captain of horse" in the conflict. The poem is built on a comparison between what happens in writing poetry—patiently seeking the right word or phrase, bringing order out of the chaos of the subconscious—and what happens in battle—waiting for the right moment to attack, subduing the chaotic forces of the enemy by an ordered advance.

Taliessin has ridden to the top of a ridge, and there he waits, his household cavalry grouped behind him. He watches, below, the pirates rush in, and Arthur's banner with the dragon on it swaying in the conflict. His cavalry grow restive; when will he give the signal to go to the king's aid? But still he waits. Sitting there on his horse, he suddenly has an inner vision of the Roman poet Virgil, standing "on a trellised path by the sea," thinking out a poem he is writing. Virgil, in his way, is also engaged in a battle, fighting to bring order and harmony into the inarticulate and half-realized ideas and images in his mind. His subconscious mind is comparable to the "sea's host" of the enemy pirates. His struggle is one that all poets know, even those who seem most spontaneous.

So Taliessin identifies himself with Virgil. Suddenly, as he waits, he sees Virgil move and take up his stylus to write, just when, in the battlefield below, a slight breach appears in the enemy ranks. Taliessin reaches for his spear at the moment that Virgil takes up his pen, and the simultaneous action of cavalry and poem is beautiful. The household soldiers seem to Taliessin, as they charge, like priests ("hierarchs") accompanying Christ, the Word; so the double action of military and poetic force takes on even more significance.

The Word, "the golden-girdled Logos," is an image taken from the Book of Revelation, where Christ is described as one with hair "white like wool" and feet "like unto fine brass." Christ the Word brings, in Revelation and in Williams's imagination, a vision of the City,[11] the place of love and coinherence. And Taliessin thinks of Virgil as also foreseeing an ideal city—Virgil who had written the *Aeneid,* the great epic of the Roman people. He thinks also of Dante, who in *The Divine Comedy* had imagined Virgil as his guide from hell toward heaven. All of this is suggested in the last sixteen lines of the poem, where the mass of marauders is broken into, and the forces of light and glory conquer the chaotic pirate force. In the lines, "the grand art mastered the thudding hammer of Thor, / and the heart of our lord Taliessin determined the war" we see the power of poetry (words in their identity with the Word) overcoming violence and incoherence. Taliessin as poet envisages the ideal City; as warrior his action is decisive in the king's victory.

"The Crowning of Arthur" shows a scene after the coronation, at the soldiers' camp just outside the wall of Camelot. The enemies have been conquered, and the occasion is one for rejoicing. It is midnight, but everyone is still awake. We feel in the background music and revelry. The glow of campfires is reinforced by that of torches and candles. The knights have put aside their weapons; their banners and heraldic shields stand massed in the yard.

Although it is a time of triumph, the poem begins quietly, with a feeling of foreboding. Merlin, the forward-looking "intelligence of time," climbs to the dome of St. Stephen's church and looks down on the colored shields glowing in the firelight. He sees Percivale's deep azure shield, Lamorack's black-banded one, Dinadan's that bears a silver dolphin, and Bors's with the symbol of charity and parental love, the pelican. Standing on his height, Merlin also "sees" Byzantium and the dome of St. Sophia, where "the kingdom and the power and the glory chimed." He knows what Logres ought to contribute to that glory. But even as he looks down on the shields, he is aware of a disturbing element: Queen Morgause of Orkney, with whom Arthur had unknowingly committed incest, leans out of a window. Evil is present. The unhappy passion of Lamorack for Morgause is also suggested, for her moon-like forehead seems to reflect the red moon on his shield.

Taliessin also knows intuitively that all is not well. He sees the shields with their representations of beasts as an image of "wildness formalized," the mathematical pattern of Byzantium civilizing the brute instincts of Logres. But something is going wrong. He is aware in the firelight of the young Queen Guinevere, and at the same moment he sees Lancelot kneel to the king. He has a vision of Arthur's heraldic dragon and Lancelot's lion locked together in conflict. What might have come about in Logres is doomed.

It is a doom made more certain by King Arthur's own attitude. We see him looking over the city, asking himself whether he is made for the kingdom, or the kingdom for him. Obviously he believes the latter, for "Thwart drove his current against the current of Merlin," and the force of his thought is felt in Byzantium: "in beleaguered Sophia they sang of the dolorous blow."

The sparks from the campfires, dying slowly away, symbolize to Taliessin the dying of the great vision of Logres. At the very moment of the king's triumph, his destruction, with that of Logres, is beginning.

Life in Logres

After "The Crowning of Arthur" *Taliessin through Logres* contains few narrative poems as such. We understand from occasional references (as in "Bors to Elayne: the Fish of Broceliande") that Arthur's kingdom is flourishing. But the story line is now abandoned. Instead, we learn what the kingdom is like and become acquainted with some of the people in it. The non-narrative poems may, therefore, be grouped roughly according to their chief ideas.

A. Love Poems.   There are love poems, beginning with "Taliessin's Song of the Unicorn," in which the unicorn is a symbol of the poet himself. He does not make an acceptable lover to most women. They find him as odd as the mythical unicorn, the beast with a single horn in his head.

The poem begins with the contrast on which it is built—between the strange, intuitive world of poetry, indicated by "Shouldering shapes of the skies of Broceliande," and the matter-of-fact, ordinary material world, the "flesh of Caucasia." The wondrous "shapes" are aspects of experience that can only be understood in myth. The unicorn, "galloped from a dusky horizon," the faintly glimpsed world of imagination, will come to a girl who beckons it, but she will not be pleased with it; it is not like an ordinary lover with whom she can sleep—its "gruesome horn" chills her, and it is altogether too alien.

Yet, Taliessin thinks, there might be that rare woman who could accept the unicorn. She would be a heroine, a holy person; the blood and tears she will shed when the unicorn's horn pierces her will be like the "twy-fount," the blood and water shed from Christ's side at the crucifixion. Her union with her strange lover will be an intellectual one, its fruit being poetry that is deep and universal ("horn-sharp, blood-deep, ocean and lightning wide").

As in other poems, Williams here equates poetry and religion. He compares the poet to Christ and the woman who accepts the unicorn to the Virgin Mary: her son will be "the new sound that goes / surrounding the City's reach"; Christ spoke of the Kingdom of Heaven, which is called the city in the Book of Revelation. The unicorn-poet also reveals the deep truth of God. It is the girl in the poem who is crucified, but then she has identified herself with the unicorn—the strange, intuitive truth that cannot be proved but is known through poetry and suffering.

A much happier love poem is "Bors to Elayne: The Fish of Broceliande." Bors, the married knight, is talking to his wife Elayne about the elusive but shiningly wonderful nature of their love. It is like a "bright-scaled, red-tailed fish" that he sees in the water. It can never be fully understood, and it cannot be summoned at will. But he knows it is both spiritual and physical ("an anagram of spirit and sense"). Perhaps, he thinks, only a "twy-nature" can understand it, like a married pair. Perhaps the Adam (Adam and Eve) knew such a love, watched such a fish "inhumanly flashing a sudden scale, / aboriginally shaking the aboriginal main." If so, the Adam knew the double nature of the fish: being physical it can redden the "happy flesh" with its tail, but at the same time it is a symbol of Christ as drawn by the first martyrs on the walls of the catacombs. Here again Williams is saying that real love is always both sensual and spiritual. Since God took on flesh, the body is holy, a temple of the spirit.

In the last three stanzas, Bors offers the fish to Elayne, as Christ offered himself to his disciples at the last supper. Bors has been made new by Elayne's love, and now he offers her back her own. It is a love that represents the inexplicable depths of Broceliande, the indefinable wild beauty that is to go to the making of the new Camelot. In some of the most beautiful lines in Williams's poetry, Bors says that Broceliande, the spirit, is everywhere inseparable from flesh. Like the substance of Logres and of Elayne herself, Broceliande "probes everywhere through the frontier of head and hand; / everywhere the light through the great leaves is blown / on your substantial flesh, and everywhere your glory frames."

In contrast to the happy, fulfilled love of Bors and Elayne and the union of flesh and spirit, there are two poems about unrequited loves and about the denial of the Incarnation and the abuse of the flesh.

The first poem, "The Coming of Palomides," tells of a Saracen knight who has come from Islam to the west. In a matter-of-fact tone, he speaks of how man is to be judged or considered. The Mohammedan system of measurement, with its symbol the curved blade, is different from the Christian one, symbolized by the cross. Mohammed's sword "cuts the Obedience from the Obeyed"—that is, divides man from God in that it denies the Incarnation. But in the "cross-littered land of Gaul" to which Palomides now comes, the "height of God-in-man" is measured by the doctrine of the Trinity ("Gospels trigonometrical") that proclaims the three-person God dwelling in every man. Palomides is skeptical of such a doctrine. He comments cynically that the Christian Church has its center at the cathedral church of Lateran, on the same hill where in earlier times the sorcerers lived. Is there any difference between magic and the "mystery" of Christianity?

But Palomides' ways of thinking are challenged when he goes to Cornwall and sees Iseult, the wife of King Mark. He falls in love with her because of her outstretched arm. His experience is rather like that of Philip in Williams's novel *Shadows of Ecstasy*. Philip looks at Rosamond's bare arm and suddenly sees in it the whole meaning of existence. So Palomides sees in Iseult the mathematical lines of the body become transfigured with spirit. Her outstretched arm is "a rigid bar of golden flame," and his "new-awakened sense" sees brightness playing around her. As he looks, he feels absolute bliss, for he is seeing a union of body and spirit, and he himself is for a moment whole. There is no conflict between his feeling and the fact of her bodily existence. He is seeing a sublime fact—she is not only beautiful but holy.

But the experience does not last. As if an "angry bolt" of lightning has struck the queen, she seems to change; he can no longer see God in her. His vision of the Trinity fades to three golden lines shining for a moment and then gone. For a short space of time he had accepted that matter (her body) was a vehicle of glory, but now his ingrained habit of keeping body inferior to mind and spirit takes over again. Her arm, that had seemed so significant, now lies "destitute, / empty of glory." Her body and spirit again seem separate.

He is aware then that she can be nothing to him. She is sitting between her husband, Mark, and her lover Tristram. And there is another entity present. Miserably, Palomides knows carnal jealousy as if it were a "questing beast," a creature that "scratched itself in the blank between / the queen's substance and the queen." Had he been able to accept the Incarnation, God actually dwelling in a body, Palomides would have known no "blank" and felt no jealousy.

In the second poem, "Lamorack and the Queen Morgause of Orkney," we are told of how King Arthur has misused the "holy and glorious flesh." In his action lies the seed of the degeneration of Camelot. The action is not told directly, but through the story of Lamorack, the knight who fell unhappily in love with Morgause, the wife of King Lot of Orkney.

Morgause is not attractive, but compelling. She seems to hypnotize men by her stony immobility; her beauty, if it can be called such, is striking and harsh. Her effect on Lamorack is convulsive and horrible; yet he cannot escape her—he falls in love.

The poem is full of images of violent action—bursting, tearing, shuddering—and of painful sounds—wailing, screaming, crying. Lamorack first sees Morgause in Orkney, surrounded by wild aspects of nature—the screaming of sea birds, the beating of waves on the shore. He sees, in a cave by the sea, "hideous huge forms," nightmarish rocks, some of which are dislodged by the storm and fly through the air. Later, when he sees Morgause sitting in King Arthur's hall, her "long eyes" remind him of the shapes in the cave.

He thinks then of another cave, or dark place, where, as Merlin told him, Arthur had committed incest with Morgause. The images of blindness used in telling of this sin indicate their unawareness of being half brother and sister, but the absence of light is horrible.

C. S. Lewis believes that Williams's chief concern in this poem is not in the psychology of Lamorack, much as he is to be pitied, but rather in the inevitable multiplying of evil, once it is sought for or thought of. When, in the myth Williams is using, Balin delivered the "dolorous blow" that wounded King Pelles, he showed the first result of the Adam's seeking to know evil. After that, Arthur sins with Morgause, and their child is Mordred, who will deliberately set out to ruin his father and all the good attempts of the knights of the Round Table. The fearsome images of this poem, says Lewis, serve to "make us feel evil not as imperfection, nor even as revolt, but as miscreation—the bringing to be of what must not (and even in a sense cannot) be, yet now it is; as though monstrous members, horns, trunks, feelers, tusks, were sprouting out of the body."[12]

In "The Sister of Percivale" we see Taliessin himself falling in love. Like Palomides on his first sight of Iseult, Taliessin suddenly sees God in a person, and his whole world is illumined. The person is Dindrane, also called Blanchefleur, who appears at Arthurs' court with her two brothers, Percivale and Lamorack.

The poem is built on geometrical images—circles and straight lines. It begins with Taliessin lying prone on the top of a wall, meditating about his poetry. A bit of summer lightning in the sky seems to indicate the coming of something unusual. But all he sees, looking down into the courtyard, is a slave girl bending over a well; her back makes a "curved horizon," and as she lifts two buckets of water, Taliessin from above sees the water as a "round plane." He also sees a scar on her back, made by a whip or sword; it flickers like the lightning. Her body seems a symbol of the Eastern Empire, with the mountains from Gaul to Caucasia. He thinks of the dangers inherent in sex. But he also knows that if her body is the East, in the other direction is the West, where lie "Percivale's duchy, Wales, and all Broceliande," symbols of spirit. Watching the movements of her body, he thinks of himself riding through mountains, over a narrow track that is the scar, riding with the evening star, symbol of Percivale's enlightenment, for his guide. The slave's eyes, as she raises herself up, show that body is always infused with spririt: "The horizon in her eyes was breaking with distant Byzantium."

At that moment a trumpet sounds at the gate, announcing Blanchefleur and her brothers. Taliessin plays with the idea that both the sound and the slave's outstretched arm are straight things but rounded gracefully.

When Blanchefleur appears, Taliessin cannot at first speak. Her beauty and radiant spirit appear to him to make complete the body of the slave girl he has just been watching. It is as if two halves of a circle came together to make a perfect whole. Taliessin has just seen a human back, and now the face, Blanchefleur's, is like God's own. Her dress, marked with lines of gold, is like a glorified depiction of the slave's scar. He is seeing divinity joined to humanity, as in Christ, and at first he is speechless. Then he leaps down from the wall and greets Blanchefleur with the words, "Bless me, transit of Venus!" He thinks of her as a heavenly body moving across the sun: she is Venus, the Third Heaven where there is absolute perfection, a union of flesh and spirit.

In Taliessin's double vision of the two girls, he has a mystical insight. Each of them represents, in his mathematical images, a horizon, a new understanding; and when both are "seen" together, the two horizons close to make the circle of understanding. The trumpet's sound had seemed to come from the bone of the slave's arm. To put it another way, "the stress of the scar" is on the same level as "the star of Percivale." Neither body nor spirit is superior to the other. They are indivisible.

A similarly complex poem, requiring careful study, is "Taliessin in the School of the Poets." It is not, strictly speaking, a love poem, but one infused with the love of God. It can be thought of as a transitional poem, leading on to the second group, poems about exchange.

Here Taliessin, as the experienced poet, talks to young poets learning the craft. His subject is the human body seen as a microcosm of the whole world. The scene is the school where the young people are at work on their own writing and also studying early forms of poetry. On the floor in front of them is a mosaic image of Phoebus, god of poetry and the sun. Taliessin's shadow falls on the golden figure as he stands in the sun. We hear the cooing of doves. All is peaceful yet charged with energy.

Taliessin begins by praising measurement, for it leads to understanding. Even the gold of butterflies' wings, he says, is put there in some exact measure. Looking down at the figure of Phoebus, he sees a human body that can be measured: it is built on two intersecting lines—the vertical of head-to-heel and the horizontal of the outstretched arms. Yet the body is more than straight lines. It glows with life; its "blossom," the mystery of its beauty, can best be understood by those with spiritual insight—those who, in a rather obscure phrase, "fly [up] the porphyry stair." This is the stair, as we learned in "The Vision of the Empire," that leads to the presence of the Emperor. It lies between earth and heaven, and those who fly up it begin to see something of the complexity of man's nature.

God's own nature, the poet says, includes every variety of thing; images of an intricately carved throne or a rich mosaic floor suggest the infinite details that make up God's love and inclusiveness. Such love must have within it "a tangle of compensations," reconciliations of the apparent contradictions of existence. And every person who lives in love finds that "Each moment there is the midmost / of the whole massive load;" that is, every moment fully lived can carry the whole of the experience of love; and wonder brings with it a will to find out more, just as sight, in this life of harmony, brings with it "direction," or instructions how to go. Such a life we saw exemplified in the character of Sybil in *The Greater Trumps*.

Taliessin then pauses to indicate that Logres has not yet reached such a state of understanding. There are still "the tribal tracks and the Roman roads" that show more primitive stages of the way.

The mention of Rome brings with it the thought of Virgil, and Taliessin quotes from Book VI of the *Aeneid*, in which the ill-fated Palinurus dies at sea before reaching Italy. In the same book Virgil describes Hades, the lower world. Taliessin's words take on a dark sadness now, as he thinks of Virgil's death and all those lost in Hades. In Hades, Virgil thought, there was no hope of resurrection, only a sad longing for the life and light left behind on earth. Such grief, too, is part of the universal pattern.

The poem ends on this double note—the young poets beginning to see the structure of the whole world, the macrocosm, indicated by "the crowned form of anatomized man," man as lord of all; and along with their eagerness, there is Taliessin's sadness. While they continue to study, in the form of Phoebus, man made in the image of God, Taliessin sighs, *"Sis salvator,* Domine," (God save us). His is the weariness and skepticism that sometimes come after one has given a lecture: though it seemed to enlighten, was it all made too simple? So much can never be explained or understood.

B. **Poems about exchange.** The mention of Virgil brings us to the poems on exchange, in particular "Taliessin on the Death of Virgil." This poem is central to all of Williams's thinking, as it presents in memorable form his idea of exchange, his basic belief that we can only be saved (from pain, suffering, and every diminishment) by other people. We cannot save ourselves. So, in the poem, Virgil's soul is saved from negation by those who have loved his poetry throughout the ages. In Williams's thought, exchange operates independently of our notions of past, present, and future.

The first stanza pictures the moment of death as a falling out of conscious awareness. As in a nightmare, everything becomes distorted for Virgil; all his life's thought and work is a chaotic jumble of noise and grotesque images. The good things he knew—the Emperor Augustus, poetry, and Rome—are now horrible. But he is keenly aware of Charon, the ferryman who carries souls to the shadowy land of Hades. In his hopelessness Virgil feels nothing to be any longer true except the being "everlastingly plucked from and sucked from and plucked to and sucked to a grave."

But he is saved from this wretched state by "unborn pieties," those not yet born when he lived, all those who found his verse a sustaining and vivifying power. They are pictured as rushing and diving to his aid, bringing him out of the void. Their love of Virgil becomes a net in which they catch him to keep him from the "endless falling." They urge him to accept their aid, as an exchange for the inspiration he has given them. So Virgil is "fathered of his friends." In the word "fathered" we feel the love and stability of God succoring Virgil. The last line, "He was set on the marble of exchange," suggests again firmness, the Psalmist's joy at being delivered out of mire and having his feet planted on firm rock.

Three other poems deal largely with the subject of exchange. "The Star of Percivale" and "The Ascent of the Spear" show how the life of exchange works among members of Taliessin's household. In the first of these, Percivale is playing the harp at early morning, and Taliessin, hearing the music, begins to sing to it. His voice is so sweet that a servant girl comes running to fall at his feet and adore him. Taliessin raises her up and tells her not to worship him, but Christ. The Archbishop, passing the girl on his way to morning mass, sees "the light of Christ's glory" in her face. Thus the love of God has been communicated by Percivale to three other people. Each of the three gives something of himself to help others. At the mass, however, there are some who have not given up selfishness. Balin, who is to deliver the "dolorous blow," feels unreasonable anger in his heart; King Arthur thinks of his own superiority; and Lancelot is thinking of Guinevere.

"The Ascent of the Spear" shows the servant girl of "The Star of Percivale" learning to accept humiliation as part of the new life of selflessness. She has been put in the stocks for attacking another slave during a quarrel. She is angry still, and miserable. Taliessin finds her and with gentle affection and understanding persuades her to recognize that she too is a sinner and to forgive the other slaves who are jeering at her. She does so and rises in spiritual stature as she is willing to discipline and humble herself.

"Bors to Elayne: on the King's Coins," in which Bors's love for his wife is this time only an incidental theme, is concerned chiefly with the life of exchange. Exchange, as we have seen, is so living in Christ that one can bear another person's burden, as Peter Stanhope bore Pauline's fear in *Descent into Hell*. But in addition to that help given to one specific person, there is also the more general life of exchange which is a consciousness of never being completely self-sufficient, but rather of living with and from others in the power of Christ.[13]

Such a life of exchange is described by Bors in the first two stanzas. He has come from London with its complex problems and sees Elayne and her women serving a meal to the farm laborers. As he watches her upright figure, her hands holding bread, she becomes a symbol of the exchanged life. The men have given their work; now they receive food. They have prepared the ground and planted grain. Now the ground gives its harvest. All of this Bors sees as being done in love, willingly, because it is the nature of things, people being members of the earth and of one another. Nobody is working "only to earn," and nobody thinks of his function as "only to pay"—there is a blessed equality in this life, each one giving more than he receives and receiving more than he gives, for Christ is sustaining and enlarging their love. Things are different in the impersonal life of London, with its "ration and rule, and the fault in ration and rule, / law and the flaw in law . . ."

What worries Bors about London is the setting up of a mint to coin money. The coins all bear the king's symbol, a dragon; and Bors thinks of dragons pouring forth all over England. Kay, the king's steward, sees nothing wrong with coining money, for "Money is the medium of exchange." Bors knows that saying, but he thinks there is danger. All goods cannot be exchanged literally of course. Money is necessary "to furnish dishes and flagons with change of food." But if people come to think of money as the only means of exchange, will they not forget the deeper obligation to be involved in others' lives? Yes! That is why Bors calls the little dragons dangerous: they "teem" on house roofs and "leer and peer" into windows menacingly. As the dragons "scuttle and scurry" across the kingdom, Bors seems to hear the City, symbol of real exchange, repeating the words of Christ, "Feed my lambs." What human concern has been neglected while a coin was tossed carelessly to the needy?

Taliessin and the Archbishop both understand Bors's fear of the coins. They see that money can give the illusion of independence, of not needing other people. Man must always be concerned for others, the Archbishop says, "for the wealth of the self is the health of the self exchanged." Money, as one means of exchange, must not be considered a substitute for the more difficult life of coinherence.

All of this Bors tells Elayne, and we feel his anxiety about Logres. When he asks if the "dead king's head," i.e., coins, can live, he is asking if Logres can ever become the joyous place of exchanged love that Taliessin had glimpsed in Byzantium.

The fourth poem in which exchange, or substitution, is important is "The Son of Lancelot," perhaps the most interesting and significant of all the poems in *Taliessin through Logres.* For here Williams deals with the birth of Galahad, showing it as heaven's way of restoring mankind after the sin of self-sufficiency known as the Fall.

It is a poem full of strong emotions, and the recurring image is that of wolves: the wolf represents passion, the force that can both create and brutalize.

The Empire, of which Logres is a part, is being surrounded by fierce alien forces; Christendom is threatened by the Moslems, who reject the Incarnation. "Over Europe and beyond Camelot the wolves ranged." Yet, even while speaking of the wolves as a threat, the poet recalls the ancient Roman Lupercalia, or wolf festival, at which priests ran about the city striking with a thong women who hoped to become more fertile. Passion can be creative as well as destructive.

In the next few stanzas we see Merlin (who is time, or history, bringing all things to pass) viewing through his magic spells the worlds of heaven and earth. His hazel wand first inscribes a circle in which he sees Europe besieged by the wolves. In the next circle is Logres, where King Arthur is thinking of himself as "Byzantium's rival" for men's worship. Next the wand moves to another scene, Taliessin reading a letter by candlelight. Then we see Blanchefleur, now a nun at Almesbury; she and her sister nuns are, in their purity, "earth's lambs," and yet they are also "wolves of the heavens," passionately devoted to God.

From earth, Merlin's wand moves to the Third Heaven of Venus, where passion is always steadfast and full. It is a place of passionate peace, a balance of forces that William Wordsworth, the "northern poet," had called the "feeling intellect." Here, as if suspended above time, Merlin hears the cries of the Roman women at the Lupercalia and at the same moment the Pope singing mass on Lateran Hill. Simultaneously there is the howl of a wolf again: this time it is a single wolf, "crouched on the frozen snow beyond Broceliande." It is the wolf that "had been Lancelot."

Merlin knows why the wolf is there, and we are now told the story: of how Lancelot had gone to Carbonek to help someone and had been persuaded to go to bed in the dark with the Princess Helayne, King Pelles' daughter, because he thought she was Guinevere. The story that in Malory occupies many lines is told here briefly and with some changes. Lancelot's union with Helayne came about through a magic spell of Brisen, Merlin's sister. It was a fated and inevitable union, for from it was born Galahad, who would restore man's ability to achieve harmony with God. The restoration would come by his healing of the wound of King Pelles.[14]

But at the time of his lying with Helayne, Lancelot knows nothing of all this. When he wakes next morning and the magic has worn off, he sees Helayne and realizes he has been unfaithful to Guinevere. Filled with remorse, he leaps out of the window and runs to the woods of Broceliande.[15] There in the woods he "grew backward" and was turned into a wolf. Even as such, though, he learns about Galahad and hates him; he begins to prowl about the region of Carbonek hoping to devour his child. He is a double creature, a man with the body and instincts of a wolf.

The poem then tells of how Galahad was born, sliding "into space, into Brisen's hands." Merlin, seeing by his wand of divination that the birth has taken place, acts immediately to take charge of the child. To do so, he deliberately transforms himself also into a wolf. The soldiers in the palace yard hear a small whistling sound as he speaks an incantation, and then they see his form grow larger, drop down on all fours, and go leaping over the snow, a white wolf. His sister Brisen hears him coming and takes the baby from Helayne's room. As Merlin approaches the castle of Carbonek, where Brisen waits, the wolf Lancelot springs upon him, but the wolf Merlin flings him off. At the door of the castle Brisen binds the baby with crimson wool to Merlin's back. Merlin lopes off with his burden and brings the child to the convent at Almesbury, where Galahad is received by Blanchefleur. There he will be reared to manhood by the nuns. Lancelot, by the force of Merlin's blow, is changed back into a man again.

This bare summary can give little idea of the richness and magic of the poem. It is Williams at his best—full of allusion and multiple meanings, but also vivid and swift-moving, written with energy and precision, and leaving the reader filled with wonder.

The story brings together several themes that were important to Williams. He felt deep sympathy for Lancelot, who loved Guinevere adulterously and yet found in that faithful love the fulfillment of something noble. Lancelot felt, Williams says in a prose essay, a conflict or contradiction between the moral sense that told him to keep away from Arthur's wife and another moral sense of "all that

was good in him" rising from that very love of the queen. Williams
quotes with approval this speech of Lancelot given by Tennyson:

> In me lived a sin
> So strange, of such a kind, that all of pure,
> Noble, and knightly in me twined and clung
> Round that one sin, until the wholesome flower
> And poisonous grew together, *each as each*,
> Not to be pluck'd asunder.

Tennyson, he says, did not develop this idea of contradiction, though
he might have found in Malory the story of how the conflict was
resolved—the story of a "holy substitution" by which Lancelot became the father of Galahad. [16]

The substitution, or exchange, of Helayne for Guinevere is for
Williams of profound significance. That it takes place without Lancelot's or Guinevere's knowledge does not matter. It is heaven's way
of using what is given—the passion of Lancelot for the queen—and
making it serve a high purpose, the bringing of Galahad into the
world. Galahad will achieve the Grail, something Lancelot is in-
capable of. He must be born of the Grail, Princess Helayne, who
symbolizes law, as Lancelot symbolizes passion. [17] Galahad comes as
Christ came, through the will of heaven, not of man.

If, then, Lancelot serves this holy purpose, why does he "grow
backward" into a wolf, trying to devour his own son? It is because
passion can also be bestial; if divorced from mind and spirit it will
deteriorate. As Merlin shows in his transformation, the human
being, capable of the feeling intellect that belongs to the Third
Heaven, can take the form of a brute that by its nature violates both
intellect and tenderness.

As we read the poem, we are aware of several actions proceeding
simultaneously, for to Williams all time was the eternal now. As
Galahad is on the point of being born, his mother Helayne feels the
"contraction and dilation" of labor, and at the same time the Empire,
the body of the world, is contracting, pressed inward by the wolves
of famine and the armies of the Moslems. It is dilating only in the
warmth of scattered "defensive fires" built to keep off the wolves.
The movement of the human body parallels that of the geographical

body. Merlin is aware of both movements. He also knows, as he prepares for his transformation, that the king is sleeping and dreaming of his own glory, and that Guinevere is tormented by jealousy and therefore growing backward like Lancelot. She has a nightmare of being in the slimy waters of P'o-lu and seeing Lancelot's figure "across the flat sea," becoming smaller and smaller as he retreats from her.

The world of the poem is very violent and very cold. Deep snows heighten the sense of isolation and fear. We see the Pope's eyes "glazed with terror" as he says mass, and "the red glow of brute famine / in the packed eyes of the forest-emerging wolves." We feel horror at Lancelot as "Slavering he crouched by the dark arch of Carbonek, / head-high howling." Merlin as a white wolf is "a loping terror, hurtling over the snow," and he strikes the wolf Lancelot with "full the force of the worlds flung."

All the more effective, then, is the contrast between this violence and the peaceful baby Galahad. As Brisen carries him downstairs to put him on Merlin's back, she calls out to Merlin, "Be blessed, brother, " and the amazing child sings "blessed brother" as it falls asleep. In the world of winter terror Galahad is secure and happy.

A similar feeling of safety after danger, due to the working of Providence in men's lives, is in the brief description of Lancelot brought back to manhood and cared for in a warm room at Carbonek: "Lancelot lay tended, housed and a man, / to be by Easter healed and horsed for Logres." The lines suggest all healing and restitution, Nature's return to life in spring, and the resurrection of the body which is one of the poem's themes. For as soon as Galahad is born, the Emperor's army begins to move to release Caucasia (the body) which had been "wholly abandoned to beast and Manichæan." If the beast is the undisciplined body and the Manichæan the denial of the holiness of the body, then Christ, as Galahad shows, comes to bring the body new honor and new life.

C. Galahad. Three other poems deal chiefly with Galahad. The first of these, "The Coming of Galahad," shows his arrival at King Arthur's court. It is a momentous occasion, for as the knights sit at their meal, the mysterious Grail appears, "a cup with a covered fitting under a saffron veil," and its power is such that, as Malory tells, each knight at the table suddenly finds he has the food he likes best. Williams thinks the change is not in the food itself, but in their minds.[18] That is, the power of the Grail brings the state of consciousness that each is ready for. They may come for the first time to an awareness of the invisible world, or God's grace.

After the feast Galahad is ceremonially conducted to Arthur's bed, where he is to sleep that night. Taliessin, standing in a lower courtyard, looks up to see "the red flares of processional torches and candles / winding to the king's bed. . . ." The picture is made vivid because of its importance: Galahad is taking Arthur's place—man's mind, symbolized by Arthur, is now supplanted by a union of mind and feeling, the Christ-like consciousness of Galahad that is a perfect balance between the head and the heart.

The greater part of the poem consists of a discussion of this necessary balance—talk by Taliessin and some of the servants as they stand in the courtyard. To Gareth, a young man who asks about the significance of Galahad, Taliessin says he represents a fitting of the "stone" to the "shell," an image that Williams takes from the fifth book of Wordsworth's *Prelude*. The stone, tougher and less delicate, signifies man's mind, and the shell his imagination or feeling. Both are needed, just as the lower courtyard, the place of the "jakes and latrines," is as necessary as Arthur's upper room. The places of "rejection and election" are both "winged shapes of the Grail's officers." Further, the balance of shell and stone can be found in five kinds of experience, which the poet calls "houses" or "cells"—the house of poetry, of the fleshly life (Caucasia), of intellect, of religion, and of mystical vision. The stone of reality can be fitted to the shell of feeling in every experience.[19]

Taliessin and the servants also talk about hands, the "winged wonder of shell and stone" which contain both feeling and action. (We recall that in *The Greater Trumps* hands are called the "instruments of spiritual intention.") Gareth has noticed that when Galahad washed his hands, the water became phosphorescent; and Taliessin explains that rare persons who are near to sanctity give forth light from their bodies. In contrast, he thinks of Queen Guinevere's hands, which, as she sat at table in her misery, looked like claws.

At the end of the poem, Taliessin has a vision of the soul coming to fruition, rising through four planetary zones to "the Throne's firmament," the highest point of heaven, or the throne of the Emperor. As Taliessin speaks of this ascent, his eyes shine like emeralds, as if they were "points of the Throne's foot that sank through Logres." Such has been the effect of Galahad's coming among them.

In "Percivale at Carbonek," we see through the eyes of Percivale how he and Bors accompanied Galahad to Carbonek, where he goes to heal the wounded King Pelles and "achieve the Grail," or realize within himself the full indwelling of Christ.

Before he enters the city, Galahad kneels down and asks pardon of his father Lancelot for his own existence. He has, by his birth, caused Lancelot to suffer. Not only did his unfaithfulness to Guinevere produce the remorse that turned him into a wolf, but even when he returns to man's form, Lancelot feels the taunt of Galahad's existence. Galahad has also distressed all of Camelot: inspired by him, knights have gone in search of the Grail and been disappointed; their departure and Galahad's achievement of the Grail mark the end of the Round Table. His purity and goodness have a double edge, wounding those who cannot understand him. The way in which nature, or ordinary life, is often outraged by sanctity is discussed by C. S. Lewis, who shows how those who follow God must often give up the life that most people know. He cites as an example Mary and Joseph seeking the twelve-year-old Jesus and finding him in the temple, when he should have been in their company on the journey home. Mary cries out, "Son, why hast thou thus dealt with us?"[20]

All of this Galahad understands, and therefore he asks forgiveness. As he kneels in the cold, his motionless figure contrasts with the "frenzy" of Lancelot that occurred in the same place. Since Lancelot is not here now, Galahad asks his cousin Bors if he can pronounce the pardon in Lancelot's name. Bors willingly substitutes himself for Lancelot and gives the pardon. Then Bors goes first into Carbonek, and Galahad and Percivale follow. They are met by angels.

The third poem of this group is "The Last Voyage." Here the same three companions, Galahad, Bors, and Percivale, sail from Logres to Sarras, the city of the soul. They are going, as it were, to the original Eden, when man was aware only of goodness and knew God's spirit within him. The three knights represent "three ways of exchange," all of them ways of giving of self and receiving blessedness. Bors does it through married love, Percivale through dedication such as monks and scholars know, and Galahad through direct mystical experience.

Also with them on board ship is the body of Blanchefleur, the sister of Percivale and Taliessin's beloved. The rays of the descending sun cover her body, lying on it like a saffron pall such as covered the Grail. She also is blessed, having exchanged her life for that of a lady who would have died but for a transfusion of Blanchefleur's blood. So tonight, we are told, Blanchefleur's spirit joins the lady, who is dancing "in the last candles of Logres."

Their ship is called "the hollow of Jerusalem," an image explained by the map of the Empire that represents a woman's body. Here Jerusalem is the womb, the place of new life. It is also the place of Christ's crucifixion. It represents a sacrifice that brings joy, or a death that brings forth life.

This "ship of Solomon" in which they sail is urged on by the Holy Spirit: a host of doves, an "infinite flight of doves," makes a supernatural wind to speed them. C. S. Lewis, commenting on the image of doves, says that the sense of speed is increased when we see the land they are leaving literally melting behind them and becoming a flight of birds.[21]

The three knights, as they sail, take statuesque positions: at the prow stands Galahad, "the alchemical Infant" who seems to glow red and then white, like some metallic substance. He sings a song of intercession for everyone in King Arthur's court. Behind him stands Percivale, like a "folded silver column"; and to their right Bors, clad in black, kneels in prayer.

Galahad's song includes Dinadan, one of Arthur's knights, who was killed by Agravaine in the wars begun by Queen Morgause's sons. The prayer is for the killers as well as the slain. As Galahad sings, he glows white, becoming Christ-like, for he is now having a direct communion with God: "in a path of lineal necessity, / the necessity of being was communicated to the son of Lancelot. / The ship and the song drove on." Even as this is happening Lancelot has come back from Gaul. Taliessin meets him at Canterbury, to tell him that Arthur has died and how King Pelles has been healed, so that "the two kings were one, by exchange of death and healing." With the Grail's and Galahad's disappearance into heaven and the end of the Round Table, Logres becomes ordinary Britain.

"The Last Voyage" is not an easy poem. It contains lines that seem needlessly obscure. In the beginning the reader may be confused, for instead of starting with the actual ship in which the knights sail, the first lines describe two painted walls of Solomon's temple, showing on one the picture of a ship and on the other Virgil giving Taliessin a hazel wand in "a laureate ceremony."

But once the voyage begins, the reader is swept along by a sense of tremendous speed. The whole atmosphere is luminous as the white doves "from the storming sky" not only follow the ship but "overfeather and overwhelm the helm," and Galahad's unearthly song seems a part of the mysterious wind that moves them. The song continues as the sun sets, and in its light the dead are as real as the living. We are no longer in the world we know—until the last stanza, when the line, "In Logres the King's friend landed, Lancelot of Gaul," recalls nostalgically the earlier poem, "The Calling of Arthur." In that poem the same line is fraught with power and purpose. Here, it reminds us that Arthur is dead, having been at war with his friend. Yet the mention of Pelles along with Arthur asures us that Galahad, the capacity for Christ in man, includes both affirmation and rejection. Though Arthur fails, Pelles is healed—they form two halves of a new unity.

   D. Palomides.   The other poems include two more on Palomides, the unhappy Saracen knight who fell in love with Iseult. In "The Coming of Palomides" we saw him become a prey to sexual jealousy when his brief vision of Iseult's spiritual nature faded. In "Palomides Before His Christening" Palomides tells of how he had hoped to catch "the questing beast" which caused the vision to vanish.

The beast is a negative thing, elusive and agile. It is unpleasant because it seems to separate the real Iseult from the woman whose sexuality is so obvious appearing "between the Queen's meaning and the Queen." Perhaps, the beast seems to insinuate, all that you felt in that vision of her glory was only sexual excitement. Perhaps lust is the only reality. If we think of Palomides as "man combatting and overcoming sex,"[22] then his struggle is with just this creature of doubt and derision, this "angel of the negative way"[23] that takes the form of a beast.

The poem shows Palomides going, in a state of despair, to Caerleon to follow a suggestion of Sir Dinadan that he be christened. His pursuit of the beast has been unsuccessful. He tells of all his failures: of how he had hoped to win honor among the knights by capturing the beast; of how everything went wrong for him—how Tristram knocked him down, and Iseult did not care; how he cheated Lancelot, who forgave him, but this magnanimous treatment did not make Palomides grateful. Rather, he became embittered by his humiliations and rode out alone to seek the beast on a barren mountain. Tired out, he rested in a cave, where his misery and introspection at last frightened him, and he determined to get out; anything would be better than this self-torment. So now he rides to find Sir Dinadan, whose gay and friendly invitation, remembered in the midst of agony, becomes a kind of compelling force.

The landscape of this poem is surrealistic, full of rocks, distorted paths, and "gaunt shapes." Palomides' jealousy of Tristram and sick longing for Iseult take on images of nightmare. On the mountain he

> clambered over house-roofs,
> without doors; on their blank sides
> the king's knights were flat cracks, chinks,
> rubbed patches, their heads grey blobs.

The lack of doors, and the "rocks . . . too hard to give any roots room" show how his seeking for self-glorification is sterile and leads nowhere. There is no spiritual growth unless one can accept defeat in the manner of Dinadan, who calls out to him as he passes, "Friend, the missing is often the catching." Palomides is in sharp contrast to Dinadan, the truly humble knight.

The cave in which Palomides takes refuge is perhaps "his own resentment and concupiscence,"[24] or perhaps, more widely, all the thoughts of his life that have brought him to this present hour. It is a terrible place, filled with greasy smoke. The questing beast lies in the doorway to the cave; Palomides no longer wants to capture it, preferring to revel in his misery. He lies on the floor, hating the air that symbolizes freedom. He has nothing left. He despairs.

But from somewhere in his consciousness there comes a change—"The sky had turned round. . . ." He remembers Dinadan and decides to go and be christened. This Christ that Dinadan speaks of is, after all, someone who became a "nothing" too. He will look a fool being christened—but why not look like a fool?

Does Palomides begin to see, faintly, what Dinadan meant by saying that "absence is a catch of the presence"—that everything is really Christ, the negation as well as the affirmation? That the questing beast is like the Skeleton in *Cranmer*—God's back? All Palomides knows with certainty is a need to go to Caerleon because of what Dinadan is—everything that he, Palomides, is not: happy, lacking self-assertiveness, detached, and somehow whole.

The second poem, "The Death of Palomides," is simple and moving. At the point of death, his mind returns briefly to the passions and desires of his life, but mainly he is filled with the memory of a night that he spent in the lodging of two old Israelites, somewhere in a mountainous district, where he heard the scream of eagles. He heard also the old men chanting songs of their religion, and one sentence returns vividly to his mind, "The Lord created all things by means of his Blessing." This he says over and over to himself, singing it in memory along with the Israelites; and it becomes the only reality.

What is the significance of this poem? Palomides has been an outsider; he has never fitted in at Logres. Rebellious, self-centered, suffering, he has not seen the significance of Galahad or known the fullness of love in exchange. C. S. Lewis says that Palomides "makes a good end."[25] But Mrs. Hadfield has a more interesting interpretation. She sees Palomides as a symbol of the self-sufficiency that must die before the new life made possible by Galahad can take over.[26] Palomides' life has been unhappy. Now, at his end, he rather reluctantly surrenders to "the kingdom, the power, the glory," and the eagles' scream that he still hears is the harsh pain of the surrender, accompanied though it be by his awareness that "Thou only art."

The End of Logres

A final group of poems gives us glimpses of the end of Logres. The first is "The Departure of Merlin." Here the magic of Broceliande, that made Logres possible, withdraws. It is no longer needed. Merlin, or time, who has been the foster-father of Galahad, has seen the young man safely in his destined place in Logres. We see Galahad, like a "joyous moon," waxing and waning in the perilous seat at the Round Table. At the same time Merlin is fading away in the sea-wood of Broceliande, meeting there at one moment Joseph of Nazareth and Joseph of Arimathea, "twin suns of womb and tomb" who are associated with the birth and death of Christ. They, too, are foster-fathers.

As C. S. Lewis points out, the poem shows two aspects of Broceliande.[27] It is beautiful, a place of fresh green leaves and vigorous growth; but it is also, being a sea-wood, in touch with P'o-lu, the place of evil. A brief, horrible picture is given of a ship sailing near Broceliande, on which one sailor, seeing the wood, "despaired of joy" and leaped overboard to his death. After he has gone, the ship moves on "on the visionary ocean track to the port of Byzantium."

Merlin does not die. He has emerged briefly from Broceliande to bring the idea of Galahad into actuality. Now he returns to become one with all moments and all growth.

The second poem is "Taliessin at Lancelot's Mass." Here "Taliessin sees the conclusion of both the Round Table and the Grail . . . Neither outward manifestation is needed now. They ascend to their true end, the worship of God in unity and joy."[28]

Lancelot, after his final parting with Guinevere, became a monk. So he is pictured here saying mass before he has been made a priest. He stands at a stone altar wearing his knight's surcoat that bears his heraldic device, the lion, but he is without sword or helmet.

Attending the mass are "all the dead lords of the Table," and in her convent Guinevere at last feels reconciled to the substitution of Helayne for herself at the conception of Galahad. Arthur and Pelles are also reconciled to events. They are shown together at the altar, Pelles approaching it, and Arthur "moving down." Arthur, through creation of the Round Table, had his part to play in the final achievement; he and Lancelot together (Lancelot as the father of

Galahad) "wove the web" of glory which appears now during the service.

In this poem of reconciliation, even Garlon, the "unseen knight" or invisible slayer who provoked the last battle, is standing with the other knights near the altar. Williams has explained that Garlon is "Satan to us but the Holy Ghost to the supernatural powers."[29] Garlon is like those other enigmatic figures who appear in Williams's plays as strange instruments of God—the Skeleton, the Third King, the Flame.

Each of the living and dead figures around the altar is both "lordlier and less" than Taliessin, who tells the story. Their talents are different, all of them contributing to the value of the whole web of glory, which is Christ's body. As they sing, it is as if a new Pentecost has come, for flames "fell from new sky to new earth."

After the Epiclesis (the invocation of the Holy Spirit) the lesson is read about the creation of man. We are made aware of how all men, not only Jesus, have God within them. Not only Mary conceives the Christ, but everyone is now capable of it, since Galahad has shown the way. Such is the suggestion in the lines, "petal on petal floated out of the blossom of the Host / and all ways the Theotokos conceived by the Holy Ghost." As the Host is held aloft, Taliessin has a vision of all opposites being reconciled around the "white rushing deck" of Galahad's ship sailing to Sarras. Then Galahad himself appears like a flame over the altar, and all who belonged to the Round Table are lifted up in light and adoration.

When the mass is over, Taliessin feels himself forever changed. What remains of his old physical self can only go back to his ordinary life in Wales. As he goes, he asks for prayers for himself and all others now dispersed into their homes.

The Region of the Summer Stars

Taliessin through Logres was published in 1938. In 1944 Williams brought out this second volume of poems, *The Region of the Summer Stars,* in which he expands some of the ideas presented in the first book. Again he deals with the Arthurian materials, and this time he is chiefly concerned with Taliessin and his household.

They are hopeful poems. By the "region of the summer stars" Williams means, briefly, an inner assurance of God's presence, arrived at after experience of suffering and evil. This region is the interior life of every real Christian. Williams has referred to it previously (in "Son of Lancelot") as the Third Heaven or place of the "feeling intellect," where all is harmony. But it can be known on earth as well. It is a consciousness of love reconciling all apparent contradictions. When one can glimpse the region of the summer stars, he knows that God's love includes all that is discordant in our experience, transmuting pain and suffering and all that we call evil into His own substance. This is the meaning of Williams's line in "The Calling of Taliessin"—[30] "the stones of the waste glimmered like summer stars." In this region we can truly see Satan as "God's shadow," as he is called in Williams's early play, *The Rite of the Passion*.[31] So, in this last of his books, we return to the chief theme of the plays, a theme that is implicit in the novels as well: evil is real on one level, and is to be combatted; but with greater understanding we see it as an instrument of God's love and a part of His purpose.

A. **The mystery of the invisible world.** As in *Taliessin through Logres,* we do not find in this book a narrative sequence, but instead glimpses of life in Logres. The book begins with a poem called "Prelude," in which the chief theme is the "twy-nature" of Christ, his showing that divinity resides in the body. Many, we are told, found this new doctrine too hard. They felt that matter could not bear the weight of spirit; they could not accept the Incarnation. But in spite of them, the Empire was established, and the faithful waited for the second coming of Christ—faith was triumphant over irony. They waited for the coming of the Grail, that single cup that would contain the essence of what was communicated meantime in the Eucharist, wherein the spiritual was brought to man by means of matter, the bread and the wine.

The whole "Prelude" is a recapitulation of Williams's belief in exchange (Christ's substitution of himself to bear the weight and punishment for man's sins) and in the importance of the Incarnation. There is an imaginative understanding of the early days of the Church, when the invisible world seemed very near: the Emperor's throne lay zoned in "clear light" that "hummed with celestial action," beings coming and going on the Emperor's business.

After the "Prelude," we are given, in "The Calling of Taliessin," the background to "Taliessin's Return to Logres" in the previous volume. The story of his birth and upbringing Williams takes from the *Mabinogion*. The child of Ceridwen, an enchantress, Taliessin is found by Elphin, who takes him out of the river Wye, where he has been left to his fate, and looks after him. The poem tells of how Elphin and his men marvel at the brightness of the baby's forehead (the name Taliessin means "bright brow") and how they sense an otherness, a transcendence about him.

As the child grows up, he explains to Elphin that he has lived forever. He appears to be the spirit of poetry, present in all times and places. As a young man he hears rumors of Byzantium, of Christ's crucifixion and resurrection, and of "the food that freed from the cycle"—possibly a reference to God's grace releasing us from the law of karma.[32] Taliessin longs to know more about this new myth, and he sets off to find Byzantium.

On his way he has to pass near the dark wood of Broceliande, on the other side of which lies Logres, not as yet established as a kingdom but a place of anarchy, "a storm of violent kings at war." He is fearful in passing by Broceliande (recalling a similar theme in "Taliessin's Return to Logres"). As he tries to steady himself, he sees ahead a shape encircled by light; it grows clearer and becomes a double shape, "gently-shining." The two shapes are Merlin and Brisen, time and space, the children of Nimue, who is mistress of the forest.

Merlin explains to Taliessin that their mission here is to found the kingdom of Logres and bring about its union with Carbonek, the seat of King Pelles, keeper of the Grail. Logres will unite in itself the Empire, a symbol of order and of unfallen man, and Broceliande, man's unruly emotional nature. Galahad, coming from Logres, will be enabled to bring the Grail, symbol of Christ in man, to the holy city of Sarras, the city of the soul. These ideas, of course, were hinted at in *Taliessin through Logres;* here they are elaborated.

The most striking part of the poem is the description of Taliessin spending the night on the edge of the wood. Half in sleep, half in vision, he sees Merlin and Brisen rise from their rest and begin a magic rite whereby the power of the Third Heaven, the region of the summer stars, is brought down to earth. They are beginning to create Logres. Taliessin sees what is happening but does not realize its full significance: "The weight of poetry could not then sink / into the full weight of glory." He sees Brisen's back become, as it were, as vast as the whole earth, and himself traveling over that earth on his way to Byzantium. Then he has a vision of the Trinity, like a point of light within a purple dusk, burning briefly until it disappears when he becomes aware of Merlin's voice telling him he must go to see the Empire.

Then he sees in Brisen's shadow Logres, lying like a flight of stairs that is also a person, with the brain at the top and the base in Broceliande's "trees and seas." Where the top, or brain, opens out into space, he sees Arthur's court; here everyone awaits the coming of Galahad. He even sees the ship that Galahad will take; on its deck stands Helayne, holding the Grail in her hands. Gradually, as the spell over him wears off, Taliessin hears Merlin instructing him to gather about himself a household of those who can understand exchange and the ways of the City. If, says Merlin, Arthur's kingdom does not last, at least the king's poet and his household "shall follow in Logres and Britain the spiritual roads." This, in fact, is what happens. But for the moment we are not thinking of the end of Logres. Morning comes on, and the three go their separate ways, "Brisen to Carbonek, / Merlin to Camelot, and Taliessin to Byzantium."

"The Calling of Taliessin" is a long, reflective poem, showing the young poet's uncertainty about his future but also his openness to all experience. His acceptance of the mystery of life leads the reader also to enter into the magical world of Merlin and Brisen and to see visions of unearthly things.

B. Poems about women.   In the next poem, "Taliessin in the Rose Garden," we have a long reflection on the nature of woman. Taliessin, walking in the garden and thinking of his poetry, sees three women at the end of a path—Guinevere, Dindrane, and a slave gardening. He does not draw near to them until the end of the poem.

The garden itself is an image of the body (he walks along "the level spinal path"); and woman, as C. S. Lewis explains this poem, represents matter, or the potential life which is given form by the sun, or by the masculine principle.[33] The flow of potential life in woman is likened to the sacrificial flow of blood from King Pelles' wound, which resulted in the quest of Galahad and therefore in a spiritual achievement.

He first sees the women among red roses. The day is still, reminding him of the tranquillity of the Third Heaven, except that here in Camelot one is aware of a seething energy coming from Broceliande, the place of making. Taliessin feels the creative energy in "the infinite and infinitesimal trembling of the roses."

The poem is full of images of red: the roses, the ruby ring of Guinevere's finger, the blood of women. The ring, as Taliessin becomes aware of it, seems to reflect or draw into itself the red of the roses—a red which can be disciplined, "the contained life of Logres-in-the-Empire," or can rush without restraint into warfare and suffering.

Like Palomides thinking endlessly of Iseult, Taliessin ponders on all women, trying to find the "zodiac in flesh," the flesh made a perfect vehicle for spirit, so that the life of exchange would be natural and practiced by all. Until that happens, he, like Palomides, feels disappointed. But even so, he has had a *vision* of perfection; in Byzantium he saw the City looking to the Emperor for its fulfillment, with Caucasia and Carbonek in perfect equilibrium—Caucasia looking to Carbonek as the City looks to the Emperor and the queen looks to the king. In Byzantium he also saw the mystery of the zodiac as it should be, each of the "houuses" or signs of the zodiac being an entry to the whole of the Empire, and all of the houses being what St. Paul calls "diversities of gifts" informed by the same Spirit.[34] He sees in Aquarius the principle of clear sight and wonders if he can see the queen as she really is; and he thinks of Gemini representing hands, and the Scorpion's sting being "controlled and ensouled in Jerusalem."

But even as he is meditating on the signs of the zodiac as symbols of spirit informing flesh, he is aware of the pattern of the whole being distorted, "botched and blotched, blood / inflaming the holy dark. . . ." He has a vision of Adam telling the Scorpion to sting and of Cain splitting the zodiac with his blow against his brother Abel. There follows the "incoherence of the houses." But at the same time Taliessin sees women everywhere, whether consciously or not, partaking of Christ's sacrifice in their monthly shedding of blood. This natural function holds within itself an image of the supernatural, and he thinks of how happy is the woman who realizes it. He wishes that Guinevere could be such a woman, but in her words to him at the end of the poem we see how far she is from the sensitivity that would make such insight possible: "the queen said, / with the little scorn that becomes a queen of Logres: / 'Has my lord dallied with poetry among the roses?' "

Two poems, "The Departure of Dindrane" and "The Queen's Servant," show something of Taliessin's relationship to members of his household. The first of these is told through the observation and thought of a Greek slave girl who must decide in a week's time whether she will remain in Taliessin's household or be freed (as the custom was after service of seven years) to go home to Athens or live her separate life in Logres. She would like to remain with Taliessin but wonders if she will always feel like that; yet she must decide now for the remainder of her life. As she broods on the situation, she sees Dindrane (Blanchefleur) depart to enter a convent at Almesbury; she is accompanied part of the way by Taliessin and some of his servants, including the Greek girl.

Dindrane's decision has not been easy; she loves Taliessin as he does her, but she has chosen to give up this dear human relationship to be a nun, giving herself wholly to Christ. Something of Dindrane's joyous energy now enters into the slave girl. She sees that Dindrane's deliberate choice of a life of service has not been imposed on her from without. Selfless service is perfect freedom—a joyful undertaking, out of love, to do the will of a beloved master. As the cavalcade rides toward Almesbury, the slave makes her decision to remain with Taliessin.

The poem is built on contrasts. Most prominent of these is that between the negative way, or the way of rejection of images, which is Dindrane's way, and the affirmative way, which is Taliessin's. Dindrane, like the bookseller Richardson in *The Place of the Lion,* chooses to know God by giving up created things and realizing only their Creator. Taliessin has chosen to live in the world of created images and find in them something more that is the Creator. Where Dindrane will do her work by prayer, Taliessin will be active in the world. As in all his writings, Williams here says that both ways are good and necessary; each expresses the abundance and generosity of God, called "largesse." A dominant theme in both volumes of poetry is the reconciliation of the two ways when Galahad, who represents the way of rejection, is born of Lancelot, who follows the way of affirmation.

The Greek girl has a mystical understanding of all this as she rides along. As soon as she knows that her choice has been made, it is as if a voice comes from the air, from the Third Heaven, saying, "fixed is the full." The words suggest wholeness, certainty, as if her choice is being confirmed by God. Then she hears "over the galloping household" another voice, that of Galahad, who has not yet been born but as a child will be brought up by Dindrane. He is sending a greeting to his father Lancelot, thus reconciling the negative and positive ways.

This awareness of the invisible world, evident also when angelic voices mingle with Taliessin's call to the cavalcade to stop, is in sharp contrast to the visible world in which the action takes place. It is a day of unceasing rain—a gray scene, suggesting departures and irrevocable decisions. One feels that the rain will go on forever; there will be no lightening of the sky, no change in the hardness of what must be endured. This hardness is seen in images of the hazel branches along the way, which represent discipline, law, and measurement. The hazel rod is also suggested by Dindrane's bare arm, "straight and strong," though the slave can also imagine the oil of dedication shining "dew-bright" on Dindrane's forehead.

The slave sees in the very rigidity of posture—the household standing motionless in the rain, Taliessin and Dindrane moving with dignity down the steps—the essence of free choice, for "Servitude is a will that obeys an imaged law; / freedom an inimaged— or makes choice of images." The decision that is made through selfless love may seem outwardly hard, like the rain or the hazel rod, but inwardly, spiritually, the person is free and happy.

This contrast between appearance and reality is evident when Taliessin calls a halt to the procession so that he may say goodbye to Dindrane. He kisses her hand and wishes her luck on the negative way, "a safe passage through all the impersonalities." She answers that she will affirm all that she should; and Taliessin says he will reject everything he should. As he then looks around, "he burned on the household," commanding them to ride with her to Almesbury and then return to Camelot. The word "burned" suggests the ardor of his love for her, which is now to be turned on the world.

The last stanza shows the slave girl before the king's bailiff, declaring her wish to remain in Taliessin's household. Now she can be "quits with those two jangling bits"; having accepted her own vocation, she no longer feels the lives of Dindrane and Taliessin as a kind of taunt or challenge. Until she makes her statement to the bailiff she has been haunted by the sound of the jangling of their harness as they all rode toward Almesbury.

In the beautiful poem called "The Queen's Servant" we see Taliessin freeing another slave girl so that she can become a servant of the queen. In doing so, he gives her new "clothes," a spiritual awareness that she will need in her new position.

The girl was bought in Caucasia; she represents the flesh or the body before the soul is mature. Now, as she is about to become free, she longs for the higher consciousness that belongs to spiritual maturity. She would like to see her native land as Taliessin does, a place of surpassing beauty, where golden-fleeced lambs frolic among roses. How, she asks him, can she gain this heightened awareness that will give her true freedom?

Taliessin says the awareness can, with difficulty, be learned intellectually. But there is a quicker way—to become nothing, indicated by the singled command to her, "Unclothe." As she obeys and stands naked before him, she represents the whole person, "fair body and fair soul one organic / whole . . ." with body as precious and as capable of salvation as soul. But only by giving up her possessions and personal desires (symbolized by her clothes) can she become a truly free person who serves God with joy, as does Dindrane when she becomes a nun. The slave's higher consciousness is symbolized by the new clothes she is to receive.

Taliessin gives her the new garments by using a magical rite, "the Rite that invokes Sarras," the city of the soul that lies beyond Broceliande. The magic he learned from Merlin, "holy, over all wizards," but it contains within it the mystery of the Eucharist. At Taliessin's command the girl stretches out her hands, and they are filled with roses that fall in a glorious heap at her feet. Next, with another chant from Taliessin,

> . . . the room grew full at once of the bleat of lambs.
> Visibly forming, there fell on the heaped roses
> tangles and curds of golden wool; the air
> was moted gold in the rose-tinctured chamber.

From the roses and wool, Taliessin creates by his magic a wonderful garment of crimson and cream color, symbols of Christ's body and blood.

We can see in this poem Williams's delight in the sensual world. The passage on the making of the garment is reminiscent of John Keats's "The Eve of St. Agnes." But within the pleasure in color and texture is the spiritual meaning. Taliessin is, in this poem, a Christ figure; he has "bought" or redeemed his people.

C. **The life of coinherence.** In "The Founding of the Company" Williams describes the beginning in Logres of what he called elsewhere[35] the "Order of the Co-inherence." This he envisaged as like other orders within the Christian church, except that it would be less tied to rules. It would consist of people everywhere who accepted and tried to practice exchange—carrying the burdens of others, and in turn allowing others to carry theirs.

In the poem it is called the "Company," which begins in Taliessin's household. It is grounded on God's original laws of love and coinherence, whereby Christ took a human body and "died man's final death for man and gave him in exchange, if man would, His own risen life to live."[36] It is based also on "the pacts of the themes," or provinces, which Mrs. Hadfield explains as "the fructiferous relationships between the parts of the empire of man, the mind and spirit and nerves and body, the conscious and subconscious . . . family bonds, the claims of religion, of country, of home, work and friends—all that goes to make up man."[37]

The beliefs of the Company are in the Trinity and the Incarnation (called in the poem the "Flesh-taking"). Its rule is "the making of man in the doctrine of largesse," which is not a hard-and-fast rule but a belief that, through Christ's coming into him, each person could live the life of "largesse," giving and receiving generously. The vow of the Company consists in each member accepting willingly that he lives "in" someone else and someone else in him—a mutual caring.

We have seen, in *Descent into Hell,* Peter Stanhope living as a member of the Company, though the term is not used in that novel. Any person, Williams believed, could join the Company at any time or place, simply by accepting and practicing its doctrine of coinherence. Undoubtedly the Company still exists among some of Williams's former students and friends, and even among those who have read his works without ever knowing him personally.

The poem explains the three kinds of members, or companions of the Order. First, there are those who willingly do the acts of exchange that always need doing in some fashion when people live together in groups. They exchange services, commodities, and money, and do so frankly and peacefully, with a feeling toward love. In the second degree are those who go a step further. They practice, when the need arises, the kind of substitution that Peter Stanhope shows when he carries Pauline's fear in *Descent into Hell.* This substitution, which Williams says has long been practiced in monasteries, is now extended to ordinary people, to anyone who agrees to take on a particular burden of another person—a friend, a fellow priest, a wife or husband.

The third station consists of "total reciprocity," practiced by those who can identify with all humanity, feeling themselves to *be* all men. "Each is mother and child, confessor and penitent, teacher and pupil, lord and slave to the other. Each is his neighbour's priest—and victim."[38] Taliessin sees that this kind of coinherence has its principle in the Trinity, whose nature (one person and at the same time three, each dwelling in the others) is meant to be followed by man so that eventually he becomes aware of "separateness without separation, reality without rift. . . ."

Having set forth the three degrees of the Order, the poem now moves to a meeting between Taliessin, walking in the rose garden, and Dinadan, one of those who live the third kind of coinherence. Dinadan greet Taliessin as the chief of the new Order, to Taliessin's dismay. He feels no better or holier than any other, and being leader would cause hellish pride, a "falling so to P'o-lu." Dinadan denies that being the chief would make for pride; somebody must be the head, and nobody is indispensable. Only God is that. Even a "God-bearer," someone like the Virgin Mary or anyone who reveals God to another, can be counted superfluous. Taliessin sees the point and agrees to be the formal head of the "unformulated Company." So the Company thrives, following the example of Christ in saving others and being saved by one another.

As a poem, "The Founding of the Company" is less compelling than some of the others, simply because of the rather difficult exposition that makes up the first part of it. There is no doubt of Williams's sincerity or of his high vision of the perfected society. Like Taliessin, he is thrilled with the idea of people everywhere living in the exchange made possible by Christ's love and self-giving. But the idea is not set forth with the vivid imagery and emotion that inform the subject in *Descent into Hell* or "Taliessin on the Death of Virgil." In a sense, "The Founding of the Company" can be thought of simply as a necessary preparation for the last poem in the book, "The Prayers of the Pope."

But before we reach the climax of "The Prayers of the Pope" there is "The Meditation of Mordred," which shows a person living in complete disregard of coinherence. Mordred, whose name suggests death, is the illegitimate son of King Arthur and his half-sister Morgause. As war has broken out between Arthur and Lancelot, Mordred has been left in charge of affairs in Logres while the king pursues Lancelot with troops in Gaul.

"I rest on his palace roof," says Mordred, suggesting in these words his lazy, irresponsible attitude toward his duties. The words also recall the *Agamemnon* of Aeschylus. That play opens with a guard lying on the palace roof waiting for the beacon fires that will announce the return of Agamemnon; but his meditation is full of unease—he has forebodings of disaster. So, making use of the same situation, of someone at home waiting on the roof, Williams has charged the poem with a feeling of doom.

Mordred has been left, he says, "the power of the kingdom and the glory"; and the irony of that phrase when used by a man who is cynical and unscrupulous shows the degradation that is setting in at Logres. Other images, too, suggest disintegration, violence, and chaos. The elms which Arthur has used to make spears for his soldiers are seen to "bud in steel points," a picture of the intolerable wrenching of the natural to the unnatural. And again trees, usually suggesting beauty, are used by Mordred to show unnatural disorder: "London is become a forest . . . / tossed caps, / towzled shouts, bare grinning leaves, / a whole wood of moral wantons. . . ."

Mordred's scorn of the Grail, which he calls a "fairy mechanism," gives the clue to his whole attitude and the reason for the decay of the kingdom. He represents all those who feel themselves self-sufficient. He, Mordred, is willing to try a little "magic" if it comes in handy, but basically he feels he needs no help. He is independent; coinherence is lost. He is pleased that Logres is no longer sending tribute to Byzantium, the spiritual city. The money, the "coined dragons" that caused apprehension in Bors ("Bors to Elayne: on the King's Coins") is now all staying at home, and Mordred reflects complacently that "I too am a dragon."

His dreams of dominance are colored by what he has heard of the Emperor of P'o-lu—cruel, arbitrary, wholly self-sufficient and decadent, living in "the green palace among his yellow seas." This is the kind of ruler that Mordred aspires to be. The images now are soft and horrible: the Emperor's wives "creep in and out"; the coolies "slink away" and "crawl with prostrations," having left a wife who did not please the Emperor to die in a cage on the edge of a swamp. Such a state Mordred would find a kind of paradise. As king, he will need nobody. When we remember the ideals of Logres, the order of the coinherence in Camelot, and Taliessin's vision of the perfected City, Mordred's desire for a solitary tyranny can only be felt as a chill of horror.

This poem differs from all the others in that it conveys no sense of the invisible world. Through Mordred's mind all has been brought down to a flat level of the seen. Instead of looking at a mosaic with its strangeness and hints of gold, we are, in reading this poem, seeing only a black-and-white photograph, clear enough but very ugly.

"The Prayers of the Pope," astonishing for its depth, its layer upon layer of meaning, forms a fitting climax to all the poems, and indeed to all of Williams's work. It holds within it and dramatizes most of his chief ideas: the importance of the Incarnation; exchange and coinherence; the affirmation and rejection of images; the vision of the City, and the relationship of good and evil. It is a solemn poem, full of an awareness of the power of evil, but also of the reality of love, which embraces and overcomes evil itself.

The young Pope, with prematurely white hair, seems "incandescent," a being full of light. Clearly he lives so completely in Christ that he is being used to bring light to the world and also to bear within his own body the evils and cruel divisions that devastate the earth.

We see him praying in the church of St. John Lateran in Rome at Christmas-time. He meditates on the Magnificat, the Virgin Mary's response to the angel's annunciation that she will bear the Christ.[39] Her reply shows her willingness to do whatever is required of her. The Pope thinks of this, and of what the birth of Christ really meant—an affirmation of an image (the new child) and also an acceptance of death, or rejection of the image:

> The young Pontiff's meditation set to *Magnificat*,
> to the total Birth intending the total Death,
> to the Love that lost Itself. . . .

Here, in "the Love that lost Itself" is the paradox that runs through the poem, the New Testament paradox that he who loses his life in unselfish service will save it.

The Pope thinks of loss—of how precious is each "image" (each person or thing, every flower or animal, house or job or other concrete good). With the loss of any image we are left "rich in sorrow," and the refrain of each of his prayers is, "send not, send not, the rich empty away." He is keenly aware of loss all around him: Logres has been destroyed in war. All through the Empire, individual themes or provinces are abandoning coinherence and set-

ting up on their own: "Frantic with fear of losing themselves in
others, / they denounced and delivered one another to reprobation."
This doctrine of every man for himself rejects the vision of the City,
where all people work in harmony.

The Pope as he prays thinks of all losses in war, and there are
wars everywhere. Barbarians from the north are invading the cities
of Gaul and stamping out civilization. The Mohammedans have
made inroads into the Byzantine Empire. Division and strife are
both within and without. The Pope's words remind us of the Nazi
myth of race during World War II (the poem was written while
Britain was being bombed), for he speaks "of myths bitter to bon-
dage, where in race / by sullen marshes separated from race / virtue
is monopolized and grace prized in schism."

But he is not just hopeless. He sees that the "enemy" is part of
himself. No man can really separate himself from others, for " 'alive
are they in us and we in them.' " The Pope offers himself as a means
of saving the broken, warring world. As he prays, he feels within
him the terrible divisions in the Empire; like a division of cells
within his body he knew that what had been identity, or mutual
service, is becoming a series of warring categories. He suffers phys-
ically, a kind of death. For he knows of Mordred's treachery to
Arthur and his scorn of the Grail. He realizes also that certain
necromancers have by their black spells raised from the dead some
poor "shapes of humanity" and forced them to march in the pagan
army. The description of them recalls passages from Williams's
novels dealing with black magic. They move in a "terrible twilight"
and the whole earth is cold at their coming.

Even as the Pope is praying, in this bleak time, for more love
in the world, a change is taking place. It seems a small thing but
is really the turning point of the poem. In the midst of what seems
despair, Taliessin, before going into battle, calls together his Company and formally dissolves it; he gives up the lieutenancy. Even
the delicate organization that the Company had is now no more,
for all are to be separated. Yet the Company itself can never vanish:
the will to coinherence, the living in and through others, will exist
in each one of the faithful. Therefore there is still hope; the healing
and restoration for which the Pope is praying will come about.

Individual members of the Company will begin, by their lives, to temper evil. The Pope prays for them, too, and for their unknown counterparts in all times and places. Like Christ's disciples, they cannot be hurt by externals; they can handle serpents without fear.

Now we witness a miracle, or rather, we see for a moment the transcendent reality that is always present. It happens through the conjunction of the Pope's prayers and Taliessin's dissolving of the Company.

First, we see the land of the Trinity, "deep heaven" or the region of the summer stars, where Bors, Percivale, and Galahad have landed after their voyage.[40] Having arrived there, they wait; they lie in a trance for a year and a day. Then the scene shifts to P'o-lu, the octopus-ridden, slimy country of evil. The tentacles of the great octopods are "slinking / and spreading everywhere along the bottom of ocean," for evil is at work, catching souls as it can. But suddenly a strange thing happens: the tentacles reach out and touch something that does not resist them—other root-like structures which are in fact the roots of Broceliande, the wood of making, the place where Taliessin met Merlin and Brisen at the outset of his career, the place of all potential good. The tentacles now find themselves held tight by the roots. They are made taut and "fixed to a regimen." By this action, evil is rendered powerless—the sorcerers and heathen gods become limp; the headless Emperor of P'o-lu sinks in the ocean and dissolves. In three memorable lines the ultimate and inevitable triumph of good is shown:

> The roses of the world bloomed from Burma to Logres;
> pure and secure from the lost tentacles of P'o-lu,
> the women of Burma walked with the women of Caerleon.

Because of this invisible action, this continuing work of the roots of Broceliande forever gripping the tentacles of P'o-lu, the Pope's final prayer takes on new power. He asks that Hell itself acknowledge the power of God. Aware within himself of the losses and divisions, and of the living dead stalking the earth, the Pope gives himself in exchange for those dead: "he offered his soul's health for the living corpses, / his guilt, his richness of repentance, wealth for woe."

Then another miracle takes place, the same one which so often goes unobserved at every communion service—the souls of those the Pope has prayed for are saved by the body of Christ:

> the Body of the Eucharist, the Body of the total loss,
> the unimaged loss; the Body salvaged the bodies
> in the fair, sweet strength of the Pope's prayer.
> The easement of exchange led into Christ's appeasement
> under the heart-breaking manual acts of the Pope.

The poor, stiff corpses of the "army" are quickly dissolved into dust. The spell of the wizards has been broken, and hope begins to revive in the war-torn Empire.

One can imagine Williams writing this passionate poem, his last, during World War II, when evil seemed triumphant and suffering was everywhere. Concerned so much with loss, the poem nevertheless asserts the positive conclusions of Williams's whole life: that every loss, though acknowledged as real and painful, can be redeemed through living in Christ, whose "Body of the total loss" rose again through the power of love. And love is shown in exchange and living by coinherence. Occasionally we will be given a vision of the transcendent power of love, as in this poem. Such moments are rare, but they can sustain us through darkness and near-despair.

Williams's Poetic Technique

The technique of Williams's poetry is unusual, reminding us now of Gerard Manley Hopkins, whose poetry he edited, and now of Anglo-Saxon poetry with its strong first beat followed by a variety of unstressed syllables. It seems rough poetry, and yet when read aloud it is surprisingly musical. Always it is striking. He wanted to get away from the too-facile, imitative verse that he had first written, through to the layers of meaning under words and phrases; and in the mature plays and poetry he uses only the new style.

The difference between his early and later style can best be seen by comparing portions of some of the Arthurian poems in *Heroes and Kings* (1930) with similar poems in *Taliessin through Logres* (1938).

We can begin with "Palomides Song of Iseult," from *Heroes and Kings,* and compare it to "Palomides Before His Christening" from *Taliessin through Logres.* The first poem is a lament for the hopelessness of the Saracen's love for Iseult. He has given up and is wholly disconsolate, saying,

> Now have I no more care
> to follow the Blatant Beast
> for the sake of Iseult the Fair;
> from all but the making of rhymes
> have I, Palomides, ceased
> in these diastrous times.

Here we note the regular rhythm and end-rhyming. In the later poem, "Palomides Before His Christening," there is no end rhyme, and the lines are of irregular length, with a strong first beat. Also, the "disastrous times" of the first poem have, in the later, been made more vivid by images of barren, rocky landscape through which Palomides climbs in a search for the Questing Beast, and by a picture of the lonely cave where he lay nursing his grief:

> Bones grew brittle; sinews yielded; spirit
> hated the air, the moving current that entered,
> movements in the cubical plot of the cave, when smoke
> emptied, and bones broke; it was dull day.

Two other portions of the same poems may be compared. The earlier poem shows the reason for Palomides' decision to go to Caerleon and be christened; he wishes to have something in common with Iseult. Again we find regular rhythm and rhyme:

> For the rulers of old are here,
> lowering over me;
> no more I fight them or fear;
> perpetually sacrificed
> I resist not their deity,
> since she was one with Christ.

His clear-cut motive in this version becomes, in the later poem, more subtle. In "Palomides Before His Christening" he leaves his smoky, bat-filled cave in desperation, needing to find something more real than his sick imaginings; and the only reality now seems to be Dinadan's invitation to come and be christened:

> At last the bats frightened me; I left
> my pretties; airy currents blew my light
> flimsy ash to the cave's mouth. There
> was the track; it went over the mountain to Caerleon.

The difference between the two versions is obvious. Where, earlier, we have easy, almost sing-song lines, in the later poem there is more compression, more reliance on imagery to suggest a state of mind, and unrhymed lines with strongly stressed beats.

A similar contrast can be seen in portions of two versions of poems dealing with King Arthur's incestuous love for Queen Morgause. The story is told in both versions by Lamorack, who also loved Morgause. Let us look at the lines in which Lamorack describes the committing of incest. In the first version, "Lamoracke's Song to Morgause," Williams suggests that Arthur and Morgause did not recognize that they were brother and sister because of the "dolorous blow," the sin of Balin that is an image of the fall of man:

> Knowledge of kinship wholly died
> and the track of the Blatant Beast ran wide,
> because of the hurt that Balin did
> when he caught to himself the Holy Thing
> and wrought upon earth a deed forbid,
> and wounded the side of the Guardian King:
> then Arthur knew not a hidden face
> but caught his sister to his embrace;
> kinship and kingship were broken laws—
> O the queen of Orkney, the queen Morgause!

In the later poem, "Lamorack and the Queen Morgause of Orkney," this becomes much more cryptic. Lamorack, sitting in King Arthur's hall, is told by Merlin that Balin, who later killed his own brother Balan, is responsible for Arthur's lack of knowledge of Morgause:

> The young wizard Merlin, standing by me, said:
> 'Balin had Balan's face, and Morgause her brother's.
> Did you not know the blow that darkened each from other's?'

Lamorack imagines the incestuous deed:

> The eyes of the queen Morgause were a dark cavern;
> there a crowned man without eyes came to a carved tavern,
> a wine-wide cell, an open grave . . .
> Through the rectangular door the crowned shape went its way:
> it lifted light feet: an eyeless woman lay
> flat on the rock; her arm was stretched to embrace
> his own stretched arm; she had his own face.

The horror of the deed is intensified by the images of darkness and blindness, together with suggestions of drunkenness and death. Yet, for all its effectiveness when we know the background, this part of "Lamorack and the Queen Morgause of Orkney" is difficult without some previous knowledge of the identity of the blind man and blind woman. The first version of the poem is much easier to understand than the second. One of the reasons for readers' difficulties with Williams's later poetry is that in reworking his original versions he often left out necessary links and explanations. He knew the background of each poem so well himself that he tended to take for granted a similar knowledge in his readers.[41]

A final example is "The Song of the Riding of Galahad" in *Heroes and Kings*, where Galahad speaks of himself, emphasizing that he is Lancelot's son:

> now I am made most bold
> to ride to King Pelleas' hold
> where is a wound to heal
>
> . . . .
>
> nor there shall it be forgot
> I also am Lancelot.

Much more effective than the rather jingling rhythm of this stanza are these lines from "Percivale at Carbonek," in *Taliessin through*

Logres, where Galahad in his joy of spiritual understanding cannot forget that he owes his physical being to Lancelot:

> Joy remembered joylessness; joy kneeled
> under the arch where Lancelot ran in frenzy.
> The astonished angels of the spirit heard him moan;
> *Pardon, lord; pardon and bless me, father.*

As these comparisons show, Williams in his mature poetry abandoned the conventional forms of his early verse. The resulting Taliessin poems are rougher, more rugged—at once more striking and more difficult.

He did not, in the later poetry, abandon stanza forms. All of the poems in *Taliessin through Logres* have a clear pattern, and the patterns are widely varied. For example, the "Prelude" contains no end rhymes and no internal rhyme, but is built on a series of threes; there are three sections, each containing three stanzas of three lines— perhaps to suggest the Trinity. Where there is end-rhyming, it is always unobtrusive. In the four-line stanzas of "The Calling of Arthur" we are hardly aware of the rhyming of the second and third lines because the poem depends for its effect chiefly on the staccato rhythm and vivid sense images.

In general, we might say that end rhymes are the least important of Williams's devices. He depends more on internal rhyme, assonance, and alliteration. In some poems we find not only internal rhyme but parallelism, which he tends to use especially when there is no regular end-rhyming, as in the following, from "Taliessin on the Death of Virgil":

> Out of the infinity of time to that moment's infinity
> they lived, they rushed, they dived below him, they rose
> to close with his fall; all, while man is, that could
> live, and would, by his hexameters, found
> there the ground of their power, and their power's use.

In the following extract from "The Last Voyage," we see both alliteration and the initial strong beat that he may owe to Anglo-

Saxon poetry; and again there is some internal rhyme and also consonance ("nature"–"creature"), as effective as assonance:

> Before the helm the ascending-descending sun
> lay in quadrilateral covers of a saffron pall
> over the bier and the pale body of Blanchefleur,
> mother of the nature of lovers, creature of exchange;
> drained there of blood by the thighed wound,
> she died another's death, another lived her life.

In these lines we can see also his use of "sprung rhythm," or one beat per foot, with the stressed monosyllables side by side—as in "saffron pall" and "thighed wound."

Just as careful study is essential to an understanding of the meaning of Charles Williams's poetry, so only by close attention to his technique can we fully appreciate the quality of his verse. We then recognize that the quick movement and complexity of his thought is expressed in a similarly delicate, complex form. Like all poetry, it needs to be read aloud if we are to hear its subtle music and follow the working of a highly original mind.

Chapter Five

His Achievement

Charles Williams's work has not achieved wide popularity—partly because it requires close attention and cannot be read with the mind slightly elsewhere. He has been considered too intellectual. Gerald Weales, in a study of modern religious drama, rates Williams as "one of the best of the modern religious playwrights"[1] because he hardly ever preaches and does not use his plays as a vehicle for propaganda; but Weales believes that secular audiences are not greatly interested in religious plays and thinks Williams's drama appeals too much to the mind and not enough to the emotions.[2]

Similarly, Father George Every finds the character drawing in the novels lacking in realism. In the early novels, he says, the characters tend to be ideas rather than people, and in the later ones they are still unsatisfactory. Simon in *All Hallows' Eve* is unreal, and characters in *Descent into Hell* are "too consciously aware of their significance in the whole supernaturally-guided pattern of events."[3] While it is true, as another critic has pointed out, that Williams cannot be judged by ordinary standards of realistic fiction,[4] many would probably agree with Father Every that such a novel as *Descent into Hell* will come in time to be classified as a spiritual classic rather than a novel, with a place on the bookshelves "with the dialogues of Plato, the *Utopia* and the *Religio Medici,* not with *Tom Jones* or *King Solomon's Mines.*" Father Every sees the novels as experiments in finding "a satisfactory medium for a modern showing of the supernatural battle," and he thinks that Williams wrote novels because he "could not yet find the kind of poetry that he needed to express all that he wanted to say."[5]

Yet the poetry, too, makes great demands on the reader's intellect. Williams has been called a philosopher-poet who did not achieve the heights because the philosophy exceeds the poetry.[6] Mrs. Ridler, who sets forth both the merits and weaknesses of Williams as a poet, says: "It is not a poetry for all moods; it is one, also, to which you must wholly submit in order to enjoy it. But I am sure that his cycle has its place in the tradition of English visionary poetry."[7] We could enlarge the scope of her statement by saying that to all of Williams's writings "you must wholly submit." Appreciating what he says does require effort.

In this connection, however, it is interesting to recall that Ruth Spalding, who produced *The Death of Good Fortune* in air-raid shelters in London during the war, said it always received breathless attention from all sorts of people. None of those crowded uncomfortably together in the shelter seemed bored. They listened to the idea presented in that play—that the energy and purpose of God are working through apparent evil to produce good—and they found sustenance in it.[8] Perhaps distress stimulates us to come to grips with basic issues and to use our minds to their full capacity. If so, in a world which still "groaneth and travaileth in pain,"[9] Williams's works will come more and more to be appreciated.

Literary reputations rise and fall; and thirty-five years—the time since Williams's death—is not long enough to say with certainty that his works will or will not last. Even if he never becomes known to great numbers, he will surely be rediscovered in each generation by those whom Arnold Bennett calls "the passionate few."[10]

He is concerned in all his writings with issues that are, or ought to be, vital to modern man. We have seen how he thinks of the relation of man's soul to God, of how the soul approaches God, affirmatively or negatively, in distress as in good fortune. Williams also considers hindrances to a knowledge of God, and all of them can be summed up as one thing: self-insistence. Not only the out-and-out villains but a number of other characters are so hindered, for example Anthony in *The House of the Octopus,* Henry Lee in *The Greater Trumps,* and King Arthur in the poetry.

The approach to God, as Williams sees it, can be through spirit or mind, for both are important, as is the body, which is a vehicle of spirit. Faith, a spiritual quality, is steady in the Archdeacon *(War in Heaven),* flickers in Cranmer *(Thomas Cranmer of Canterbury),* and is strong in the Pope in *The Region of the Summer Stars.* Two who approach God through the mind or reason are Lord Arglay in *Many Dimensions* and Anthony in *The Place of the Lion.*

Williams gives much attention to the problem of good and evil. To him evil is a necessary accompaniment to being human—but nonetheless it is to be always resisted. Hence the power struggle so prominent in the novels. Sometimes power inheres in a magical object that is sought for by opposing groups, but power can also, as in *All Hallows' Eve,* be a swaying of other people to one's own will. Only in *Descent into Hell* is the power struggle absent; there, the emphasis is turned to exchange and the life of coinherence.

As a critic points out, Williams's concern is always with the *uses* of power. In itself, power is neutral and can be either used or abused: "Those who receive power without seeking, . . . and exercise it in humility and charity, become beneficent super-beings. . . . Those, however, who snatch power and try to use it for their own ends become monsters and destroyers."[11] Mrs. Hadfield reminds us that in the early twentieth century material power was still being glorified and moral standards were rapidly changing; Williams used themes that were popular in a time of fluctuating and uncertain values, but he transformed these themes:

Power, personality and sex fill his novels—but with what a difference! They are the starting point for him instead of the finishing post. His stories start at power and lead out to freedom and peace and love; they start at personalities and lead out to coinherence and unity; they start at sex and lead out to the full nature of matter and the body in glory.[12]

Evil must be combatted, but ultimately, Williams believes, it is powerless. What power it has is derived from good and a distortion of good. His plays make the point clearly. His symbolic characters— the Skeleton *(Cranmer)*, the Accuser *(Judgement at Chelmsford)*, the Flame *(The House of the Octopus)*, and the Third King *(Seed of Adam)*— are his most significant contributions to religious drama. At first these characters seem to contradict all we have thought about a tender, loving God. With their consent Cranmer and Anthony are brought to frightful deaths, and Chelmsford is painfully humiliated. The Third King comes on the scene as an evil threat, attended by Hell.

Yet all of them represent God—aspects of God that seem evil to mortal eyes. Williams is saying that God may reveal Himself not as help and comfort but as "contradiction and entire dismay," a description of Satan in an early play, *The Rite of the Passion* (1929)[13]; in that play Satan is also called "God's shadow." The Skeleton tells Cranmer that he is "Christ's back." (54) The Accuser represents judgement, not usually thought of as pleasant; and the Flame, though readily available to man, can burn as well as enlighten.

The Third King provides an indication of the relation of evil to God. He tells Adam that even before man was created, Eden contained hunger and living things "with a need always to feed on each other" (170) in order to have relationship. The possibility of choosing hunger existed from the beginning and therefore derived from God. But when one makes this choice, he is at the same time choosing to see only God's back (an adverse condition or evil), for relationship holds the possibility of greed, hate, murder. Good continues to exist but is no longer recognized.

In the novels, also, evil is good distorted or seen awry. Sir Giles Tumulty in *Many Dimensions* cannot recognize the splendor of the light that shines around Chloe because he can no longer see good. The light to him is fearful and menacing, and it finally destroys him. In *All Hallows' Eve* the rose-colored light coming from the heart of love appears to Simon as burning and horrible. Palomides in the poems must dimly see, at the end, that the questing beast is "God's back," for he dies admitting that "Thou only art." Tumulty and Simon are not given this grace, for they never loved anyone but themselves and cannot see even the shadow of love. In the novels, evil is something that inevitably dwindles, shrinks, and becomes as nothing in the face of the splendid, apocalyptic power of the good.

In his struggle against evil or in his feelings of isolation, man is never alone. Williams sees him as supported by invisible presences, which sometimes actually reveal themselves. So St. Osyth in *Judgement at Chelmsford* has a vision of the City of coinherence; Jonathan in *All Hallows' Eve* sees the City and paints a picture of it that inspires Richard. Sybil in *The Greater Trumps* sees Christ, the Fool, and in *War in Heaven* Prester John appears to strengthen those toiling after good. In Williams's last two novels God's spirit is not embodied in a character but felt as a force by Lester *(All Hallows' Eve)* and Pauline *(Descent into Hell)*.

It is in the poetry, especially, that we see the power of God as a reality. "God writes straight with crooked lines," says a Portuguese proverb. In the poems we see how He uses what is given, the love of Lancelot and Guinevere, and transforms it—Galahad is born to help man find Christ within himself. Also, though Camelot falls, the reality of exchange has been firmly established in the minds of Taliessin and his Company, and in our minds. We think of Virgil being saved by readers who lived centuries after him; of Blanchefleur being substituted for a woman who was ill; of Arthur exchanged for Pelles in "Taliessin at Lancelot's Mass," and the Pope substituting himself for suffering mankind in "The Prayers of the Pope."

The poems abound in positive images. Praise breaks forth just after a melancholy description of the fall of man ("The Vision of the Empire"); references to Christ remind us that he redeemed the self-seeking of Adam; the figure of Galahad moves as a glowing presence throughout the cycle of poems. The region of the summer stars, or the Third Heaven, symbolizes a new consciousness, a heightened awareness of the love that reconciles all contradictions.

The strangeness or unique quality of the imagery in Williams's poetry has been commented on by C. S. Lewis and other critics. Mrs. Ridler says that he gains his unusual effect "by the close linking of abstract and physical terms: 'times variously veined', 'the fine air of philosophical amazement', 'mystical milk', 'hair bleached white by the mere stress of the glory', and so on."[14] He uses images both as symbols and as suggestions of ideas or states of mind, or linking one level of experience with another. For example, the "heaped roses" and "golden wool" of the slave girl's dress ("The Queen's Servant") suggest the Eucharist, a means of making all things new.

Even when his sense images seem chiefly important in creating atmosphere, there is a faint other-worldly feeling about them. When Percivale describes Galahad kneeling at the gate of Carbonek, ("Percivale at Carbonek") the scene is not only cold but rather unearthly:

> Between the Infant and Bors and myself on each hand
> under the arch I heard the padding of paws,
> woven between us, and the faint howl of the wolf.
> The High Prince shivered in the cold of bleak conjunction.

But for all its strangeness, the world of Charles Williams is not fantasy. His writings are not "escape" literature; instead, they show us how wonderfully exciting our own world is if we really see it. They open up unheard-of vistas in the commonplace. His is a realism, says William Lindsay Gresham, "which concerns itself with essences instead of surfaces." He continues:

Most fantasy makes its effect by exploiting the antithesis between the Natural—seen as the "real," commonplace, everyday world—and an unreal Supernatural. But Williams's point is that the Natural *is* the Supernatural. The bread and wine *are* the body and blood of God—what else could they be? And reading him we feel like the blind man who was given his sight and saw people like trees walking. [15]

It is the world we know that Williams shows us, but heightened by his vision and insight. In his world there is a sense of order and purpose. We see it in the novels and plays when evil is overthrown by means of man's cooperation with God. In *Seed of Adam* Hell is constrained to fall down and worship God. Cranmer's soul is saved almost in spite of himself *(Thomas Cranmer of Canterbury)*. Pauline fulfills her destiny and eases the painful death of her ancestor *(Descent into Hell)*. Examples could be multiplied. No matter how chaotic the world seems, its affairs are directed by God.

Like the plays and novels, the poems, too, for all their romantic turbulence and occasional obscurity, have throughout a feeling for pattern, design, or order. It comes partly from the frequent references to straightness or to the hazel wand: "the nuts of the uncut hazel fall / down the cut hazel's way," says Taliessin to the young poets he is instructing, suggesting that the natural sense of order (the uncut hazel) is reinforced in Logres by the self-discipline symbolized by the cut hazel wand ("Taliessin in the School of Poets"). Merlin enters the region of the summer stars by means of his wand of "straight and sacred hazel" ("Son of Lancelot"). Taliessin, riding into Arthur's camp, finds it bordered by hazels: the new regime in Logres is intended to follow God's plan for bringing peace and order into a troubled kingdom ("Taliessin's Return to Logres").

There is, throughout the writings, a feeling of joyous energy or exhilaration, which is linked to the discipline or purpose just mentioned. We think of the vigor of the novels, with event crowding upon event; of Taliessin's joy in finding his place in the world, and of the night he spends on the edge of Broceliande and in the "illumined dusk" learns of Merlin's and Brisen's plan to establish Logres; of Galahad's joy as he sails to Sarras. We remember the energy of Merlin when as a white wolf he bounds over the snow carrying the baby Galahad on his back, fulfilling a sacred purpose ("The Son of Lancelot"). Especially in "The Son of Lancelot" and "The Prayers of the Pope" Williams makes clear that nothing can permanently interfere with the working out of God's plan and will for good, for light and life.

With these poems in mind, we can appreciate the burning intensity of the climax of "Taliessin at Lancelot's Mass," where the soul of Taliessin seems to leave his body and rejoice with Galahad and all the dead knights of the Round Table. He becomes for that moment transfigured in glory:

> joy to new joy piercing from paths foregone;
> that which had been Taliessin made joy to a Joy unknown;
> manifest Joy speeding in a Joy unmanifest.

This is like the Archdeacon's death in *War in Heaven*—a scene quiet but full of vitality. Both scenes express an idea we have noted in all of Williams's work: the constant presence of the invisible world, which now and then pierces through a cloud or veil and shines into our everyday lives.

Notes and References

Chapter One

1. Alice Mary Hadfield, *An Introduction to Charles Williams* (London, 1959), p. 13. Most of the biographical facts of this chapter are based on Mrs. Hadfield's book, hereafter cited as Hadfield.
2. Humphrey W. B. Carpenter, *The Inklings. C. S. Lewis, J. R. R. Tolkien, Charles Williams and their friends* (London: Allen & Unwin, 1978).
3. Mark 15:31.
4. Margaret Sinclair, "The Making of *The House of the Octopus,*" unpublished lecture to the Charles Williams Society, London, November 25, 1978.
5. William Blake, "I rose up at the dawn of day," *The Complete Writings of William Blake,* ed. Geoffrey Keynes (London: Oxford University Press, 1966), p. 558.

Chapter Two

All page references in the text are to *The Collected Plays by Charles Williams,* ed. John Heath-Stubbs (London, 1963).

1. Gerald Weales, *Religion in Modern English Drama* (Philadelphia, 1961), p. 106.
2. Ronald C. D. Jasper, *George Bell: Bishop of Chichester* (London: Oxford University Press, 1967), pp. 42–43.
3. Weales, pp. 107–21.
4. Introduction to *The Image of the City* by Charles Williams (London, 1958), p. lvii.
5. In his essay, "The Cross," *Image of the City,* p. 134.
6. John Heath-Stubbs, *Charles Williams* (London, 1955), p. 15.
7. Charles Williams, *He Came Down from Heaven* (London, 1950), p. 30.
8. Ibid., pp. 31–32.
9. "Religious Drama," *Image of the City,* pp. 55–56.
10. Ibid., p. 57.

11. Ibid., p. 55.

12. *Oxford English Dictionary,* Definition of substance, Sense 3.

13. Psalm 118:26.

14. John 2:4.

15. Cf. Christ's being born of a virgin.

16. John 15:15.

17. John 14:1.

18. Introduction to *Four Modern Verse Plays* (London: Penguin, 1966), p. 12.

19. *Collected Plays,* p. 174.

20. It was written for 1939, the year of the anniversary, but could not be performed until after the war, by which time Williams had died.

21. *He Came Down,* pp. 19–22.

22. Ibid., p. 43.

23. Matthew 26:47.

24. George Every, *Poetry and Personal Responsibility* (London: SCM Press, 1949), p. 46.

25. Heath-Stubbs, Introduction to *Collected Plays,* p. xii.

26. Ibid.

Chapter Three

All page references in the text are to the Faber & Faber edition of the novels.

1. Williams identifies Ideas with the qualities that make up people, see p. 64 below.

2. Revelation 12:7–8.

3. Henry Yule, "Prester John," *Encyclopaedia Britannica,* 9th ed.

4. Cf. Luke 23:43

5. Matthew 27:42. Mark 15:31.

6. Canto 25.

7. See Genesis 2:9.

8. Alfred Douglas, *The Tarot* (Baltimore: Penguin, 1973), pp. 13, 15.

9. Ibid., p. 51 and *passim.*

10. Ibid., pp. 108–109. The two children figure on the Tarot card.

11. "Lilith," *The Oxford Companion to English Literature,* 1933.

12. Hadfield, p. 174.

13. Edmund Fuller, *Books with Men behind Them* (New York, 1962), p. 227.

14. Hadfield, p. 143.

Chapter Four

1. Charles Williams and C. S. Lewis, *Arthurian Torso* (1948, reprinted, London, 1969).
2. Hadfield, p. 146.
3. Mary McDermott Shideler, *The Theology of Romantic Love* (Grand Rapids, Mich., 1966), p. 102.
4. Anne Ridler, Introduction, *Image of the City,* p. liii.
5. Hadfield, p. 146.
6. "The Poetic Achievement of Charles Williams," *Poetry* 3, 11 (September–October, 1947): 44–45.
7. Circe is a character in Homer's *Odyssey,* an enchantress who could transform men into beasts. For Comus see Milton's poem of that title.
8. Charles Williams Society Newsletter, no. 6. (Summer 1977), Supplement 2, p. 1.
9. *Arthurian Torso,* p. 109.
10. Charles Williams Society Newsletter, no. 7 (Autumn 1977), Supplement 3, p. 1.
11. Revelation 1:14–15; 21:10–27.
12. *Arthurian Torso,* p. 132.
13. See "The Founding of the Company," *The Region of the Summer Stars.*
14. Charles Williams, "Notes on the Arthurian Myth," *Image of the City,* pp. 175–79.
15. In Malory this drastic action takes place some months after the event but Williams sees the dramatic value of making it occur immediately.
16. *The English Poetic Mind* (Oxford, 1932), pp. 191–92.
17. Williams, "Notes on the Arthurian Myth," *Image of the City,* p. 177.
18. Williams, "Introductory Note to the Arthurian Essays," *Image of the City,* pp. 171–72.
19. Hadfield, pp. 152–53.
20. *Arthurian Torso,* pp. 174–76.
21. Ibid., p. 179.
22. Williams, "Notes on the Arthurian Myth," *Image of the City,* pp. 176–77.
23. Every, *Poetry and Personal Responsibility,* p. 46.
24. *Arthurian Torso,* p. 165.
25. Ibid., p. 173.
26. Hadfield, p. 153.
27. *Arthurian Torso,* p. 172.
28. Hadfield, p. 154.

29. Williams, "Notes on the Arthurian Myth," *Image of the City,* p. 178.

30. In *The Region of the Summer Stars.*

31. Williams, *Three Plays* (London, 1931), p. 190.

32. Lewis, in *Arthurian Torso,* p. 98.

33. Ibid., p. 147.

34. 1 Cor. 12:4.

35. Postscript to *The Descent of the Dove,* p. 236.

36. Hadfield, p. 160.

37. Ibid.

38. Lewis in *Arthurian Torso,* p. 143.

39. See Luke I:46–55.

40. See "The Last Voyage" in *Taliessin through Logres.*

41. Anne Ridler, Introduction, *Image of the City,* p. lxiv.

Chapter Five

1. Weales, *Religion in Modern English Drama* (Philadelphia, 1961), p. 274.

2. Ibid., pp. 142–64.

3. George Every, "The Novels of Charles Williams," *S.S.M. Quarterly* 53, 182 (September, 1952): 40.

4. W. R. Irwin, "Christian Doctrine and the Tactics of Romance. The Case of Charles Williams," *Shadows of Imagination* (Carbondale: Southern Illinois University Press, 1969), pp. 142–43 and *passim.*

5. Every, "The Novels of Charles Williams," pp. 38–40.

6. "The Philosopher-Poet," *Times Literary Supplement,* February 6, 1959, p. 51.

7. Ridler, Introduction, *Image of the City,* p. lxxi.

8. Personal interview with Ruth Spalding, February 19, 1976.

9. Romans 8:22.

10. Arnold Bennett, *Literary Taste* (London: Frank Palmer, 1909), pp. 23–27.

11. Irwin, "Christian Doctrine and the Tactics of Romance," p. 140.

12. Hadfield, p. 80.

13. Williams, *Three Plays,* p. 142.

14. Ridler, Introduction, *Image of the City,* p. lxvi.

15. William Lindsay Gresham, "The Nature of Reality," review of *The Place of the Lion, Saturday Review of Literature,* March 24, 1951, p. 14.

Selected Bibliography

PRIMARY SOURCES

1. Biography
Bacon. London: Arthur Barker, 1933.
James I. London: Arthur Barker, 1934.
Rochester. London: Arthur Barker, 1935.
Queen Elizabeth. London: Duckworth, 1936.
Henry VII. London: Arthur Barker, 1937.

2. Drama
The Masque of the Manuscript. London: Henderson and Spalding, 1927.
A Myth of Shakespeare. London: Oxford University Press, 1928.
The Masque of Perusal. London: Henderson and Spalding, 1929.
Three Plays. London: Oxford University Press, 1931. Contains *The Witch, The Chaste Wanton,* and *The Rite of the Passion.*
Collected Plays. Edited by John Heath-Stubbs. London: Oxford University Press, 1963. Contains *Thomas Cranmer, Judgement at Chelmsford, Seed of Adam, The Death of Good Fortune, The House by the Stable, Grab and Grace, The House of the Octopus, Terror of Light,* and *The Three Temptations.*

3. Literary Criticism
Poetry at Present. Oxford: Clarendon Press, 1930.
The English Poetic Mind. Oxford: Clarendon Press, 1932.
Reason and Beauty in the Poetic Mind. Oxford: Clarendon Press, 1933.
The Figure of Beatrice. A Study of Dante. London: Faber and Faber, 1943.
"The Figure of Arthur." *Arthurian Torso: Containing the Posthumous Fragment of* The Figure of Arthur *by Charles Williams and a Commentary on the Arthurian Poems of Charles Williams by C.S. Lewis.* London: Oxford University Press, 1948. Reprint 1969.
The Image of the City and Other Essays. Edited by Anne Ridler. London: Oxford University Press, 1958.

4. Novels

War in Heaven. 1930; reprint London: Faber and Faber, 1947.
Many Dimensions. 1931; reprint London: Faber and Faber, 1947.
The Place of the Lion. 1931; reprint London: Faber and Faber, 1952.
The Greater Trumps. 1932; reprint London: Faber and Faber, 1954.
Shadows of Ecstasy. 1933; reprint London: Faber and Faber, 1948.
Descent into Hell. London: Faber and Faber, 1937. Reprint 1955.
All Hallows' Eve. London: Faber and Faber, 1945. Reissued 1947.

5. Poetry

Heroes and Kings. London: Sylvan Press, 1930.
Taliessin through Logres and *The Region of the Summer Stars*. New Edition
    London: Oxford University Press, 1954.

6. Theology

He Came down from Heaven and *The Forgiveness of Sins*. London: Faber and
    Faber, 1950. Reprint 1956.
The Descent of the Dove: A Short History of the Holy Spirit in the Church.
    London: Longmans, Green, 1939. Reprint New York: Meridian
    Books, 1956.
Witchcraft. London: Faber and Faber, 1941. Reprint New York: Meridian
    Books, 1959.

SECONDARY SOURCES

In the annotations, Charles Williams is designated by C. W.

Eliot, T.S. Introduction to *All Hallows' Eve* by Charles Williams. New
    York: Pellegrini and Cudahy, 1948. Discussion of C. W.'s familiarity
    with the supernatural world.
Every, George. "The Novels of Charles Williams." *S.S.M. Quarterly* 53,
    182 (September, 1952): 37–43. A fair and interesting summary of
    the strengths and weaknesses of the novels.
Fuller, Edmund. *Books with Men behind Them*. New York: Random House,
    1962. Discusses power, substituted love, and the City as themes in
    C. W.'s novels.
Glenn, Lois. *Charles W. S. Williams. A Checklist*. N.p.: Kent State Uni-
    versity Press, 1975. Indispensable guide to all C. W.'s works and to
    works about him.

Hadfield, Alice Mary. *An Introduction to Charles Williams*. London: Robert Hale, 1959. Clear, concise treatment of his life and works; essential for serious students of C.W.

Heath-Stubbs, John. *Charles Williams*. London: Longmans for the British Council, 1955. One of a series, "British Writers and Their Work," this is a brief but valuable account of influences on C.W., his leading themes, and his achievement as a novelist, dramatist, and poet.

————. Introduction to *Collected Plays by Charles Williams*. London: Oxford University Press, 1963. Helpful background notes and commentary on the nine plays included.

————. "The Poetic Achievement of Charles Williams." *Poetry* (London) 4 (September, 1947): 42–45. Discusses C. W.'s use of myth in the Taliessin poetry and his indebtedness to other poets such as Yeats.

Irwin, W. R. "Christian Doctrine and the Tactics of Romance. The Case of Charles Williams." In *Shadows of Imagination*. The fantasies of C. S. Lewis, J. R. R. Tolkein and Charles Williams, edited by Mark R. Hillegas. Carbondale: Southern Illinois University Press, 1969. A discussion of the novels of C.W.

Lewis, C. S. "Williams and the Arthuriad." In *Arthurian Torso*. London: Oxford University Press, 1948. Reprint 1969. Lewis has, with scholarly insight and understanding of C.W.'s thought, made valuable comments on each of the Taliessin poems.

Moorman, Charles Wickliffe. *Arthurian Triptych. Mythic Materials in Charles Williams, C. S. Lewis, and T. S. Eliot*. Berkeley: University of California Press, 1960. Discussion of C. W.'s purpose and method in his Arthurian poetry.

Ridler, Anne. Introduction to *The Image of the City and Other Essays by Charles Williams*. London: Oxford University Press, 1958. A perceptive, valuable commentary on C. W.'s life and his ideas as they appear in his novels, drama, criticism, and poetry.

Sayers, Dorothy Leigh. "Charles Williams: A Poet's Critic." In *The Poetry of Search and the Poetry of Statement*. London: Victor Gollancz, 1963, pp. 69–88. Chiefly concerned with C. W.'s critical study of and similarity to Dante, but also giving general comments on C. W.'s personality and thought.

————. Introduction to *James I* by Charles Williams. London: Arthur Barker, 1951. Vigorous comment on all of C. W.'s work, emphasizing his originality.

Shideler, Mary McDermott. *The Theology of Romantic Love. A Study in the Writings of Charles Williams*. Grand Rapids, Mich.: William B. Eerdmans, 1962. Examines the pattern of ideas underlying C. W.'s work, especially his theory of romantic love as leading to the love of God and the world. Thorough and helpful.

Spanos, William V. *The Christian Tradition in Modern British Verse Drama: The Poetics of Sacramental Time.* New Brunswick: Rutgers University Press, 1967. Discusses the Christian vision of C. W., T. S. Eliot, Christopher Fry, and others—their emphasis on the Incarnation and their sacramental view of life and time.

Weales, Gerald. *Religion in Modern English Drama.* Philadelphia: University of Pennsylvania Press, 1961. Discusses the use of religion on the commercial stage, giving a fair assessment of C. W.'s achievement in drama.

Index

Charles Williams is designated C.W.